The Scientific Quest for the World's Funniest Joke

The British Association for the
Advancement of Science

ARROW

Published by Arrow books in 2002

Copyright © The British Association for the Advancement of Science 2002

The right of The British Association for the Advancement of Science to be identified as the author of this work has been asserted by them in accordance with the Copyright, Designs and Patents Act, 1988

Arrow Books Limited
The Random House Group Limited
20 Vauxhall Bridge Road, London SW1V 2SA

Random House Australia (Pty) Limited
20 Alfred Street, Milsons Point, Sydney, New South Wales 2061, Australia

Random House New Zealand Limited
18 Poland Road, Glenfield, Auckland 10, New Zealand

Random House South Africa (Pty) Limited
Endulini, 5a Jubilee Road, Parktown, 2193, South Africa

The Random House Group Limited Reg. No. 954009

www.randomhouse.co.uk

A CIP catalogue record for this book is available from the British Library

Papers used by Random House are natural, recyclable products made from wood grown in sustainable forests. The manufacturing processes conform to the environmental regulations of the country of origin

Design & make up by Roger Walker

Printed and bound in Great Britain by
Cox & Wyman Limited, Reading, Berkshire

ISBN 0 09 944687 1

For further information about the BA and its work please contact
The BA, 23 Savile Row, London W1S 2EZ
Telephone: 020 7973 3500
www.the-ba.net

We have excluded jokes that were attributed to specific comedians and writers, or obtained permission from the person concerned to reproduce his or her material. If anyone can prove the authorship and/or copyright ownership of any of the jokes, we will gladly acknowledge them in future editions, or remove the jokes from the text.

Acknowledgements

LaughLab was created from an idea by Dr Richard Wiseman from the University of Hertfordshire.

The LaughLab team consisted of Sue Hordijenko, Nick Hillier, Jill Nelson and Steven Chapman from the British Association for the Advancement of Science, and Dr Richard Wiseman, Dr Jed Everitt, Meyric Rawlings, Emma Greening and Helen Large from The University of Hertfordshire.

LaughLab was carried out as part of Science Year, and we would like to thank Andy Yeatman from The Met Office, Caroline Watt and Clive Jeffreys for their invaluable help with the project. Special thanks to comedian Tim Vine for his permission to reproduce his jokes on pages 116, 129 and 138. Finally, our special thanks to the hundreds of thousands of people from all around the world who were kind enough to participate in the experiment.

*laugh*LAB

What lies on the bottom of the ocean and quivers?
A nervous wreck.

Submitted by Douglas from Edinburgh, age 8.

A family of tortoises went into a cafe for some ice
cream. They sat down and were about to start eating
when father tortoise said: 'I think it's going to rain.
Junior, will you pop home and fetch my umbrella?'
So, off went Junior for father's umbrella, but three
days later he still hadn't returned. Eventually, the
mother tortoise said to the father tortoise: 'Dear, I
think that we had better eat Junior's ice cream before
it melts.'
And a voice from the door said: 'If you do that I won't
go.'

Submitted by Caroline from Chicago, age 31.

Customer: 'Waiter, waiter! How do you prepare your
chickens?'
Waiter: 'Oh, nothing special – we just tell them
straight out that they are going to die!'

Submitted by Norman from London, age 55.

I've been married fifty four years today, and I'm still in
love with the same woman – if my wife finds out,
she'll kill me.

Submitted by John from Los Angeles, age 74.

Introduction

In September 2001 we embarked on one of the world's largest, and most unusual, scientific experiments. The aim of the project was to find the world's funniest joke, and answer important questions about the psychology of humour at the same time. For example:

Do men and women find the same jokes funny?
Does our sense of humour change as we grow older?
What is the best time of day to tell a joke?
Do people from different countries laugh at the same jokes?

The experiment was called LaughLab and was carried out as part of Science Year in the UK. The idea was very simple. We established an Internet site containing two sections. In the first section, people submitted their favourite jokes. In the second section, people answered a few simple questions about themselves – such as whether they were male or female, young or old, and which country they were from – and then rated how funny they found a random selection of jokes that had been submitted by others.

The experiment captured the imagination of individuals throughout the world. We received thousands of jokes and had them evaluated by hundreds of thousands of people.

At the end of the project, we carefully examined all the information and discovered the gags that made men giggle and women groan, those that tickled children but not adults and the jokes that proved most popular in different countries. Along the way we also uncovered the 'winning' jokes in many different categories, including the best 'doctor' jokes and funniest 'man walks into a bar' gags. After much hard work, we finally managed to track down the world's best and worst jokes.

This book contains the results of our record-breaking experiment – both the jokes themselves and the amazing insights they reveal about what makes us laugh and why.

So sit back, have fun and discover what happened when serious science put jokes and laughter under the microscope.

Welcome to

.co.uk

The launch of LaughLab

We launched LaughLab in September 2001 at The British Association for the Advancement of Science's Festival of Science in Glasgow, Scotland. The response from the media was amazing. The following day, LaughLab was reported all around the world – in newspapers and magazines, on television and radio, and all over the Internet. Thousands of people flocked to LaughLab, and helped start the experiment by submitting their favourite jokes.

Within 24 hours, we had collected over five hundred jokes. Obviously we couldn't allow any offensive jokes on to the site, so each and every joke had to be vetted. This job was carried out by LaughLab team members Helen and Emma. Within days, they had lost their sense of humour and gained probably the finest collection of rude jokes anywhere in the world.

Within a week, over ten thousand people had logged on to the site, all eager to read our first set of jokes and tell us how funny they found them.

The mathematics of mirth

People indicated how funny they found jokes in LaughLab by using our special Giggleometer:

Once people had read a joke, they chose one of the five faces to indicate the extent to which it made them groan, grin or guffaw. We then calculated a 'Joke Score' for each gag – this was the percentage of times that people awarded the joke a rating of '4' or '5' on the Giggleometer.

To explain how this worked, let's select two jokes at random from the LaughLab database.

Joke A   Patient: 'Doctor, I think I'm a pair of curtains.'
             Doctor: 'Pull yourself together man.'

Joke B   One day, a trucker was driving some penguins to the zoo. Suddenly, his truck breaks down and he is forced to stop at the side of the road. He flags down a farmer in a van and says: 'I'll give you £100 if you take these penguins to the zoo.' The farmer accepts, loads the penguins into the back of his van and drives off. A few hours later, the trucker is still trying to fix his truck when the

farmer drives past with the penguins still in the back of his van. The trucker shouts out: 'Hey, I thought I gave you £100 to take those penguins to the zoo!' 'Well, I took them to the zoo,' says the farmer, 'but then I had some money left over, so now I'm taking them to the cinema.'

Let's imagine that one hundred people read joke A, and that five people awarded it a '4' rating and another five people gave it a '5' rating. Overall, this joke would have been rated as either '4' or '5' by ten people, and therefore received a Joke Score of 10% (10 ÷ 100 multiplied by 100).

Now let's imagine that Joke B has also been rated by one hundred people. However, this joke is seen as much funnier than Joke A, and twenty people awarded it a '4' rating and another thirty people awarded it a '5' rating. This joke would therefore receive a Joke Score of 50% (50 ÷ 100 multiplied by 100).

So, the funnier the joke, the higher the Joke Score.

The first 500

To give you an idea of the relationship between the Joke Score and the jokes themselves, here are some of the Joke Scores for the best and worst of the first 500 jokes submitted to LaughLab.

All these jokes obtained a Joke Score of about 2%, indicating that they produce little more than the tiniest of titters.

What is the sleepiest fish?
A kipper.

What time is it?
Time you got a new watch.

What is black and white and red all over?
A used newspaper!

What is black and white and eats like a horse?
A zebra.

What do you call a fly with no wings?
A walk.

Why do cows have bells?
Because their horns don't work.

Some of the best of the first 500 jokes

The following jokes obtained Joke Scores in the 30% to 40% range, indicating that about a third of people found them funny.

This guy is walking past a wooden fence. On the other side of the fence is an asylum. The inmates are all screaming at the tops of their lungs: 'Thirteen! Thirteen! THIRTEEN!!' The guy notices a small hole in the fence and his curiosity naturally gets the better of him. He takes a peek and a finger suddenly pops out and jabs him in the eye. He yells in pain as the inmates start shouting: 'Fourteen! Fourteen! FOURTEEN!!'

A truck driver saw a priest hitchhiking and thought he would do a good turn. He pulled the truck over and said: 'Father, I'll give you a lift, climb in the truck.' The happy priest climbed into the passenger seat and the truck driver continued down the road. Suddenly, the truck driver saw a lawyer walking down the road and instinctively swerved to hit him. But he remembered that there was a priest in the truck with him, so at the last minute he swerved back, narrowly missing the lawyer. Even though he was sure he missed the lawyer, he still heard a loud 'THUMP'. He glanced in his mirrors but didn't see anything. He then turned to the priest and said: 'I'm sorry Father, I almost hit that lawyer.' 'That's okay,' replied the priest, 'I got him with the door!'

Two hikers were walking through the woods when they noticed a bear charging towards them in the distance. The first hiker removed his trail boots and began to lace up his running shoes. The second hiker laughed and said: 'Why bother changing out of your boots? You can't outrun a bear.' The first hiker replied: 'I don't have to outrun the bear, I only have to outrun you.'

A man from Chicago has to go to Las Vegas to attend a one-day business conference, and has arranged for his wife to fly down and join him after the conference finishes. When he arrives at his hotel, he decides to send a quick message to his wife back home. Unable to find the piece of paper on which he wrote her e-mail address, he does his best from memory. Unfortunately, he doesn't get it exactly right and the message is routed to someone whose husband recently passed away. When the grieving widow opens her e-mail, she takes one look at her monitor, screams and faints. The message on the computer screen read:

> 'My darling wife . . . just checked in, everything is prepared for your arrival tomorrow. Looking forward to us being together again.
> Your loving husband. P.S. It sure is hot down here.'

The search continues

The response from the public continued to amaze us. Thousands of people logged on to LaughLab from all around the world, many of whom were eager to submit their favourite joke. Others were kind enough to answer questions about themselves – such as their age, what country they were from, whether they were male or female – and, perhaps most importantly of all, indicate how funny they found some of the jokes in the LaughLab database. Within just a few months, we had collected thousands of jokes and hundreds of thousands of ratings.

At the end of December 2001, we decided to carry out an initial analysis of the data. We carefully examined all the information that we had collected, and identified the best and worst joke at that time.

There was a huge difference in the Joke Scores of the two jokes. The worst joke had received a Joke Score of just 1% – almost the lowest score possible. The best joke had obtained a Joke Score of 48% – indicating that nearly half of the people that had read it had awarded it either a '4' or '5' rating on the Giggleometer.

The worst joke was an old classic:

Why did the chicken cross the road?
To get to the other side.

Grrrooooooaaaaaaannnnnnn!!!!!!

And the best joke was:

Sherlock Holmes and Dr Watson were going camping. They pitched their tent under the stars and went to sleep. Sometime in the middle of the night Holmes woke Watson up and said: 'Watson, look up at the stars, and tell me what you see.'

Watson replied: 'I see millions and millions of stars.'

Holmes said: 'And what do you deduce from that?'

Watson replied: 'Well, if there are millions of stars, and if even a few of those have planets, it's quite likely there are some planets like Earth out there. And if there are a few planets like Earth out there, there might also be life.'

And Holmes said: 'Watson, you idiot, it means that somebody stole our tent.'

A top jokester

The Holmes and Watson joke was submitted by Geoff Anandappa, from Blackpool in Britain. We contacted him and told him the good news. He was delighted and kindly agreed to be interviewed by journalists on the day that we announced our results. Here's his account of that rather unusual day:

On the day the announcement was made I was staying with friends near Portsmouth. I received a call from my father in Blackpool, saying that people from the newspapers, radio and television had been trying to contact me! The calls continued all day, much to the amusement of my friends. I did loads of newspaper and radio interviews. The lady from The Sun *was a bit disappointed – I was a bit too boring for them, I think!*

Then a newspaper photographer turned up with a Sherlock Holmes kit, which he'd found in a joke shop! We spent two hours in my friends' kitchen, with their kids holding up the photographer's lights, and me trying not to look like a complete idiot!

Next, I started getting phone calls and e-mails from friends all over the world, saying they'd seen my picture in their local papers! Friends sent me cuttings from Malaysia, Sri Lanka, Australia, New Zealand, Borneo . . . Almost all my friends worldwide had heard the story, either on television or radio or newspaper. It was amazing.

More people join the quest

Our 'winner so far' announcement encouraged even more people to join in the experiment. Thousands more jokes poured in from all four corners of the world on just about every possible topic. Long jokes and short jokes, good jokes and bad jokes, clean jokes and dirty jokes. Helen and Emma continued to vet each and every one.

Within a few months we received thousands more jokes, and over three-hundred-thousand people told us about themselves and how funny they found the jokes. We collected massive amounts of data and LaughLab eventually became one of the largest experiments ever conducted.

The final analysis of the data unraveled the mystery of what makes us laugh and why.

The remainder of this book contains the results of our massive experiment and answers lots of interesting questions about humour. What was the top 'doctor' joke? And which was the winning 'man walks into a bar' gag? Why do we find some jokes funnier than others? Do men and women have a different sense of humour? Do people from different nationalities share the same sense of humour? Did Holmes and Watson continue to lead the pack or were they pipped to the giggle post by another top gag? All will be revealed.

Throughout the book we have also included lots of fun facts about laughter, some of the surprising results from other research into humour and famous quotes concerning comedy.

laughLAB

So hold on to your sides and get your giggling gear ready for action, as we delve into the first set of LaughLab results . . .

Top 'doctor' jokes

We received hundreds of jokes involving doctors. We examined the Joke Score of every one and identified the top ten. As with all the lists in the book, they will appear in reverse order.

 A guy walks up to the receptionist in the psychiatrist's office and says: 'I'm the Invisible Man and I'd like to talk to the doctor.' The receptionist pokes her head into the psychiatrist's office and says: 'There is a man here who wants to talk to you, and he claims he's the Invisible Man.' The psychiatrist replies: 'Tell him I can't see him right now.'

 A doctor says to his patient: 'Without these treatments, you've got three months to live' and hands him a bill. The patient says: 'My God! Look at all these. I can't come up with this kind of money in three months!' The doctor says: 'All right! You've got six months to live.'

Patient: 'Doctor, when I press my stomach it hurts, When I press my cheeks it hurts, and when I press my leg it hurts! What's wrong with me? Is it serious?'
Doctor: 'No, it's just your finger that is broken!'

 Patient: 'Doctor, doctor, I can't pronounce my Fs, Ts and Hs.'
Doctor: 'Well, you can't say fairer than that then.'

 Patient: 'Doctor, doctor, I can't get this song out of my head and it's driving me mad. I can't stop humming "It's Good to Touch the Green Green Grass of Home".'
Doctor: 'Hmm, sounds like Tom Jones Syndrome.'
Patient: 'Never heard of it.'
Doctor: 'Well, it's not unusual . . .'

 The doctor says to the patient: 'You're in excellent health – you'll live to be ninety.' The patient replies: 'But doctor, I am ninety!'
The doctor responds: 'Well, that's it then.'

4 A man walks into a doctor's surgery and says:
'Doctor, my legs keep talking to me!!'
The doctor says: 'Don't be daft, let me have a listen.'
He puts his ear to the man's thigh and it whispers:
'Lend us a tenner.'
Amazed, he moves down to the knee and it whispers:
'Give us a fiver.'
Astounded, he moves to the calf, which says: 'Give
us a quid.'
Perplexed, the doctor refers to his medical journal,
and finally says: 'I can see the problem – your leg is
broke in three places.'

3 A man goes to the doctor and says: 'Doctor, there's a
piece of lettuce sticking out of my bottom.' The
doctor asks him to drop his trousers and examines
him.
The man asks: 'Is it serious, doctor?' The doctor
replies: 'I'm sorry to tell you, but this is just the tip of
the iceberg.'

2 A man goes to the doctor and has a check up.
The doctor says to his patient: 'I have bad news and
worse news.'
'Oh dear, what's the bad news?' asks the patient.
The doctor replies: 'You only have 24 hours to live.'
'That's terrible,' said the patient, 'How can the news
possibly be worse?'
The doctor replies: 'I've been trying to contact you
since yesterday.'

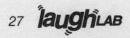

But LaughLab's award for the top 'doctor' joke goes to:

The doctor gives a patient a check-up and looks very
concerned.
Patient: 'Okay doc, break it to me, how long do I have
to live?'
Doctor: 'Ten.'
Patient: 'Ten what? Years? Months?'
Doctor: '. . . nine . . . eight . . . seven . . . six . . .'

Laughter really is the best medicine

Research suggests that laughter is good for our health.

One of the most important parts of the body's defenses against disease and illness is its immune system. Experiments suggest that people who laugh more, and are able to look on the funny side of life, have healthier immune systems than others.[1]

A good laugh also increases our heart rate, helps us breathe more deeply, and stretches many different muscles in our face and upper body. In fact, it is like a mini work-out – a quick visit to the giggle gym. And the effects are far from trivial. One researcher estimated that a good laugh produces an increase in heart rate that is equivalent to ten minutes on a rowing machine or fifteen minutes on an exercise bike.[2]

Other researchers have found that people who suffer from heart disease are 40% less likely to laugh or see the funny side of life. As Dr Michael Miller, director of the Centre for Preventive Cardiology at the University of Maryland Medical Centre in Baltimore, said: 'We know that exercising, not smoking and eating foods low in saturated fat will reduce the risk of heart disease. Perhaps regular, hearty laughter should be added to that list.'

So, when it comes to our health, the consequences of not laughing could be deadly serious.

 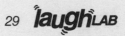

'I laughed until it didn't hurt'

Research also shows that laughter can help reduce pain.

In the best-selling book, *Anatomy of an Illness (As Perceived by the Patient)*, Norman Cousins described how he used laughter to overcome the pain of arthritis. Cousins reported how ten minutes of laughing at Marx Brothers films could lead to over two hours of pain-free sleep. His experiences have now been supported by years of medical research.

Research with rheumatoid arthritis sufferers has shown that laughter helps relieve both the intensity of pain, and the degree to which patients find such pain bothersome.[3] And a survey of dentists revealed that patients who laughed more in their lives experienced less pain during dental surgery than less-humorous patients.[4]

But why should laughter reduce pain? One theory concerns the link between laughter and chemistry. Endorphins are a special chemical produced by our bodies to help reduce the effects of pain and handle stress. Some researchers believe that laughter produces endorphins which, in turn, help to deaden the effects of pain.

Top 'God' gags

We had lots of jokes about God and other divine entities. After analysing the Joke Score for each one, we can now reveal LaughLab's top four God gags.

 A man prays to God every night: 'Oh God, let me win the lottery.' This goes on for weeks until eventually a voice booms from the heavens and says: 'Come on, meet me halfway here – at least buy a lottery ticket!'

 A shipwreck survivor washes up on the beach of an island and is immediately surrounded by a group of native warriors.
'I'm done for,' the man cries in despair.
'No you are not,' comes a booming voice from the heavens. 'Listen carefully, and do exactly as I say. Grab the spear from the one who is beside you and shove it through the heart of the chief.'
The man does so, and the remainder of the band stare in disbelief.
'Now, what?' the man asks the heavens.
'Now, you are done for.'

 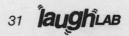

2 A flash flood swept over an area, stranding a man in his house. As the water rose, a rescue team came by in a boat.

'Get in,' the rescuers said. 'We'll take you to safety.'

'No,' said the man, 'I have faith in the Lord. He will save me.' The rains continued and soon the man was forced up on to his roof to avoid drowning.

Soon, another boat came by.

'Sir, please get in,' the rescuers in this boat said. 'The waters are rising. We'll take you to safety.'

'No,' said the man again, 'I have faith in the Lord. He will save me.' The boat left, and soon the man was barely able to keep his head above the water.

The water became rougher and a helicopter was dispatched to save the man. 'We'll lower a rope. Get in the helicopter!' yelled the rescuers from above. 'The water shows no sign of abating. You're sure to drown!'

Once again, the man refused. 'I have faith in the Lord,' he said calmly. 'He will save me.'

Eventually, the man drowned. When he got to heaven, he saw the Lord and approached him. 'What happened?' asked the man. 'I had faith that you would save me from drowning. Why didn't you?'

'Hey,' replied the Lord. 'I sent two boats and a helicopter. What more did you want?'

And the winning God gag is:

A guy gets home from work one night and hears a voice. The voice tells him: 'Quit your job, sell your house, take your money, go to Vegas.' The man is disturbed at what he hears and ignores the voice.

The next day when he gets home from work, the same thing happens. The voice tells him, 'Quit your job, sell your house, take your money, go to Vegas.' Again the man ignores the voice, though he is very troubled by the event. Every day, day after day, the man hears the same voice when he gets home from work: 'Quit your job, sell your house, take your money, go to Vegas.' Each time the man hears the voice he becomes increasingly upset.

Finally, after two weeks, he succumbs to the pressure. He does quit his job, sells his house, takes his money and heads to Vegas. The moment the man gets off the plane in Vegas, the voice tells him: 'Go to Harrah's.' So, he hops in a cab and rushes over to Harrah's. As soon as he sets foot in the casino, the voice tells him: 'Go to the roulette table.' The man does as he is told. When he gets to the roulette table, the voice tells him: 'Put all your money on 17.' Nervously, the man cashes in his money for chips and then puts them all on 17. The dealer wishes the man good luck and spins the roulette wheel.

Around and around the ball goes. The man anxiously watches the ball as it slowly loses speed until finally it settles into number . . . 21.

The voice says: 'Damn.'

 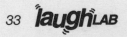

This winning joke was submitted by Paul, a 44 year-old professional symphony orchestra musician from Caracas, Venezuela. We emailed him and asked him how he discovered it and why he liked it:

The joke came to me as a daily e-mail joke. The irony of the image of God (or something God-like) as a compulsive gambler, playing with an ordinary Joe's life, just struck me as very amusing, so I tell it to everyone I know, even people I don't like.

Wit is educated insolence.

ARISTOTLE

Philosophers and scientists have been fascinated by humour for over 2000 years. The famous philosopher, Aristotle (384–322 BC), wrote a great deal about the topic. Unfortunately, we only have indirect references to his ideas because his actual treatise on laughter has been lost in the mists of time.

Interestingly, it is this lost volume of humour that lies at the centre of the well-known book and film *The Name of the Rose*.

When scientists laugh

Because we were conducting a scientific experiment, we approached some of Britain's best-known scientists and science writers and asked them to tell us their favourite jokes for LaughLab.

Here are the best of their submissions:

A brain and a jump-lead go into a pub. The brain orders two pints from the barman, but the barman refuses to serve him. When asked why, the barman replies: 'Well, you're clearly out of your head, and your friend looks as if he's about to start something.'

Dr Heather Couper – Astronomer and broadcaster

How do you catch a polar bear?
You cut a hole in the ice and you put peas all around the edge. When the polar bear comes along and stops for a pea, you kick it in the ice hole.

Professor Colin Pillinger – Planetary Scientist,
Open University

Two cows are in a field. One turns to the other and says: 'Daisy, I'm worried, I'm afraid we've got mad cow disease.'
Daisy replies: 'Oh, there's nothing to worry about, we're giraffes!'

Professor Steve Jones – Evolutionary biologist,
University College London

And it didn't stop there:

The Queen of Potatoes asks her three daughters to search the kingdom looking for suitable husbands. The princess potatoes travel far and wide and eventually return with the names of the potatoes that they would like to marry. The first princess potato says: 'Mummy, I would like to marry King Edward.'
'Well done,' says the queen, 'a very suitable choice.'
The second princess potato says, 'Mummy, I would like to marry Jersey Royal.'
'Well done again,' says the queen, 'another very suitable choice.'
The third princess potato says, 'Mummy, I would like to marry Desmond Lynam.'
'You can't marry him,' says the queen.
'Why not?' asks the disappointed princess.
'Because he's a common 'tater!'

Dr Simon Singh – Science writer and author of The Code Book

A woman dies and, at the funeral, her lover is crying. Her husband comes up to him and says: 'Please don't worry, I will marry again soon.'

Professor Lewis Wolpert – Professor of Biology as Applied to Medicine, University College London

And even more:

What's the difference between a shopping trolley and a University Vice-Chancellor?
You fill them both up with as much food and alcohol as you can, but it's only the shopping trolley that has a mind of its own.

Professor Sir Howard Newby – Sociologist, President of The British Association for the Advancement of Science, 2001–2002

What's an ig?
An Eskimo's home with no toilet.

Baroness Susan Greenfield – Neurobiologist, Oxford University. Director of the Royal Institution

Hear the tale of Frederick Worms, whose parents
    weren't on speaking terms:
Now when Fred wrote to Santa Claus, he wrote in
    duplicate, because
One went to dad and one to mum – each asking for
    plutonium.
The lumps met in Fred's stocking, and laid waste
    some ten square miles of land.
Learn from this tale of nuclear fission: never mix
    science with superstition!

Adam Hart-Davis – Television science presenter

Is it true that cannibals don't eat clowns because they taste funny?

Dr Richard Wiseman – Psychologist, University of Hertfordshire

Top joke by a scientist

The winning joke in this category was submitted by Professor Harry Kroto, Nobel Laureate Professor of Chemistry at the University of Sussex:

> A man walking down the street sees another man with a very big dog.
> One man says to the other: 'Does your dog bite?'
> The man replies: 'No, my dog doesn't'.
> The man pats the dog and has his hand bitten off.
> 'I thought you said your dog didn't bite,' said the injured man.
> 'That's not my dog,' replied the other.

In addition to his Nobel prize, Professor Kroto can now boast of being a LaughLab winner!

 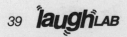

Gigglebytes

A few years ago, Dr Graham Ritchie and Dr Kim Binsted created a computer programme that could produce jokes.[5] We were keen to discover if computers were funnier than humans, so entered five of the computer's best jokes into LaughLab. Three of them received some of the lowest Joke Scores in the entire database! Here are those failed puns:

> What kind of contest can you drive on?
> A duel carriageway.

> What kind of line has sixteen balls?
> A pool queue.

> What kind of pig can you ignore at a party?
> A wild bore.

However, two examples of computer comedy were surprisingly successful and beat about 250 human jokes:

> What do you call a ferocious nude?
> A grizzly bare.

> What kind of murderer has fibre?
> A cereal killer.

So, jokes written by a computer are not particularly funny to humans, but perhaps they would be hilarious to other computers.

Top 'science' jokes

We also received lots of jokes with a science theme. Here are the top ten:

 10 What do you get when you divide the circumference of a pumpkin by its diameter?
Pumpkin pi!

 9 Why can't a scientist tell a joke timing.

 8 Some tourists in the Chicago Museum of Natural History were marvelling at the dinosaur bones. One of them asked the guard: 'Can you tell me how old the dinosaur bones are?'
The guard replied: 'They are three million, four years, and six months old.'
'That's an awfully exact number,' says the tourist. 'How do you know their age so precisely?'
The guard answered: 'Well, the dinosaur bones were three million years old when I started working here, and that was four and a half years ago.'

 7 What do you tell a mathematician on a Saturday night?
Don't drink and derive.

 6 'Sally, can you spell 'water' for me?' the teacher asked.
'H I J K L M N O,' answered Sally promptly.
Her teacher looks puzzled: 'That doesn't spell 'water'!'
'Sure it does,' said Sally. 'It's all the letters from H to O!'

 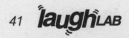

5 Three American-Indian women in the wild west are about to give birth. One is lying on a buffalo skin, one is lying on a moose skin and one is lying on a hippopotamus skin. The first woman gives birth to a boy. The second gives birth to a girl. And the third gives birth to a boy and a girl. And this proves . . . the squaw of the hide of the hippopotamus is equal to the sum of the squaws of the other two hides!

4 Two statisticians went duck hunting. Not being very good, they did not see a duck all day. Just as they were about to leave, a duck flew out in front of them. Both aimed and fired. One shot went two metres to the left of the duck, the other two metres to the right, and the duck escaped. However, they went home very happy, because, on average, they had hit the bird!

3 An engineer, a physicist and a mathematician are on a train in Scotland. The engineer looks out the window and sees a black sheep. He comments: 'Look, they have black sheep in Scotland.'
The physicist looks and comments: 'From this observation, we can only say there is at least one black sheep in Scotland.' The mathematician then looks and comments: 'Actually, from this we can only say there is at least one sheep in Scotland that's black on one side.'

2 A neutron walks into a bar and says: 'Give me a beer.' The bartender says: 'Hey! Neutron! For you – no charge!'

And the winning 'science' joke is:

> Two atoms were talking. One atom said to the other:
> 'Why are you crying?'
> The atom replied: 'I've lost an electron.'
> The first atom said: 'Are you sure?'
> 'Yes,' replied the other. 'I'm positive!'

This was submitted by Richard, 27, a project manager from Birmingham in Britain.

I think I heard the joke on the radio, I love 'pun type' jokes, so this just fits my sense of humour – simple but highly effective! The joke appeals to me because I am a technical person who loves gadgets and science, but I also love great humour – my biggest comedy heroes are people like Eddie Izzard, Billy Connelly, Phil Kay, Dave Gorman . . . so just silliness floats my boat!

Where do jokes come from?

In a short story entitled *The Jokester*,
science-fiction writer Issac Asimov
outlined a rather strange idea to account
for the origin of jokes.[6]
The story is set in a futuristic world in which
almost any question imaginable can be answered by a
massive computer called Multivac. The main
character in the story has the job of creating new and
interesting questions for the computer. He notices
that although everyone knows a few jokes, nobody
ever claims to have actually created them. Eventually,
he becomes so fascinated by the origin of jokes that
he asks Multivac to tell him where jokes come from.
After millions of calculations and much deliberation,
the computer eventually reveals that jokes have been
planted in our minds by an extraterrestrial force as
part of a huge cosmic experiment into humour.

This realisation then causes the experiment to
terminate, so that nobody in the world can think of
any jokes, or even remember what a joke is.

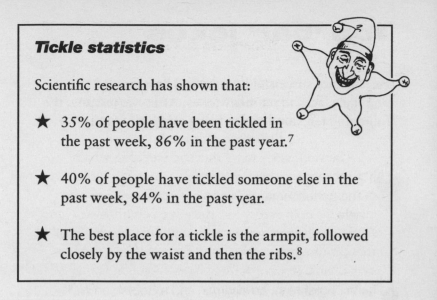

Tickle statistics

Scientific research has shown that:

★ 35% of people have been tickled in the past week, 86% in the past year.[7]

★ 40% of people have tickled someone else in the past week, 84% in the past year.

★ The best place for a tickle is the armpit, followed closely by the waist and then the ribs.[8]

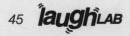

Top 'bar' jokes

Perhaps not surprisingly, pubs and bars proved to be popular places to set many jokes. After the judging, the following ten stood out as being especially funny.

 A mushroom walks into a bar.
The bartender says: 'Hey we don't serve your kind here.'
The mushroom replies: 'Why not, I'm just a fun guy!'

 An Englishman, an Irishman and a Scotsman walk into a bar. The barman says: 'Is this a joke?'

 Two pieces of tarmac go into a pub and boast to the barman about how hard they are: 'We're motorways us.'
Then another piece of tarmac enters and the first two hide under a table.
'What's wrong?' says the barman: 'I thought you were really hard?'
'We are,' they say. 'But he's a cycle path.'

A woman walks into a bar, orders a double entendre, and the barman gives her one.

 A man walks into a pub, and asks the barman for a pint of beer. While waiting for his drink, he notices that Vincent Van Gogh is sitting at one of the tables. He goes up to him and says: 'Are you Vincent Van Gogh?'
'Yes,' the old man replies.
'Do you want a pint?' says the man.
'No, thanks,' says Vincent. 'I've got one 'ere.'

 Shakespeare walks into a pub. The bloke behind the counter says: 'I'm not serving you mate – you're Bard.'

 Charles Dickens walks into a bar and orders a Martini. The bartender asks: 'Olive or Twist?'

We had two variations of the joke that made it into third place . . .

3 A grasshopper walks into a bar. The bartender says: 'Hey, we have a drink named after you!'
The grasshopper replies: 'Why'd you name a drink Bob?'

Or

A white horse goes into a pub and orders a drink. The publican says: 'Here, we've got a drink named after you!'
The horse says: 'What, Eric?'

2 Two jelly babies walked into a bar with their friend the hard gum. When they went up to get drinks, some cough sweets went up to them and started hassling them. The jelly babies were a bit scared and went to the hard gum to ask for a bit of help. He replied: 'I'm not going anywhere near them, they're menthol!'

But the winning 'bar' joke was:

A man walks into a bar and orders a pint. Then he hears little voices saying things like: 'Oooh, you look really nice' and: 'That haircut really suits you.'
He tells the barman about it, and the barman says: 'Just ignore it, it's the peanuts – they're complimentary.'

Punch lines

We didn't want to include any jokes in LaughLab that were offensive or rude. However, we thought it might be fun to show you some of the punch lines from some of the jokes we excluded, and leave the rest up to your imagination.

And the vicar said: 'I don't mind kissing the chimpanzee, but I am not touching that banana.'

'I tried that,' said Susie, 'but the next night he came to bed with some lettuce and olive oil.'

The man beams and asks why. The woman answers: 'So I can get it enlarged!'

After the laughter had subsided, the teacher glared at the student and said: 'That's not an excuse, you can use your other hand to write.'

And one of the men responded: 'No, it's just that we usually use the camel to ride into town.'

Find the missing joke – five more punch lines for those with a wild imagination

So the guy leans over to the frog and says: 'All right, I'm only going to show you how to do this one more time!'

The man replies: 'No, it's just frost on my moustache.'

To which the other crew member replies: 'Yeah, you can have a go every day except Thursday.' Confused, the new guy asks why, and receives the reply: 'Because it's your turn in the barrel on Thursday.'

'Well,' said the barman. 'I don't know how he does it, but it's the same every night. He walks in, orders a drink, and just sits there licking his eyebrows...'

And the vicar quickly replied: 'Couldn't she just have eaten the parsnip?'

Men and women, introverts and extroverts, left and right-handers

We asked people taking part in LaughLab to tell us whether they were:

Male or female

Introvert or extrovert

Left or right-handed

Overall:

Females found the jokes funnier than males.

Extroverts found the jokes funnier than introverts.

Left-handed and right-handed people found the jokes equally amusing.

Top joke chosen by right-handers

A man lay sprawled across three entire seats in a
theater. When the usher came by and noticed this he
whispered to the man: 'Sorry, sir, but you're only
allowed one seat.'
The man groaned but didn't budge.
The usher became impatient. 'Sir,' he said, 'if you
don't get up from there I'm going to have to call the
manager.'
Again, the man just groaned, which infuriated the
usher, who turned and marched briskly back up the
aisle in search of his manager. In a few moments,
both the usher and the manager returned and stood
over the man. Together the two of them tried
repeatedly to move him, but with no success. Finally,
they summoned the police.
The cop surveyed the situation briefly. 'All right buddy,
what's your name?'
'Sam,' the man moaned.
'Where you from, Sam?' the cop asked.
'The balcony,' replied the man.

Top joke chosen by left-handers

A parachutist is doing his first freefall jump. As he falls, he remembers everything he has to do as he reaches the various altitudes. At the proper altitude, he pulls the cord. Nothing happens! He pulls again. Nothing! He pulls the emergency cord. Nothing! Almost in a panic state he tries to remember what the instructor said about this situation but he can't remember anything. He is resigned to dying on his first freefall. He looks down in a sort of ghoulish curiosity to see where he is going to thunder in. He sees something he can't understand. It looks like something coming up to meet him. As it gets closer, he recognizes a female figure wearing a cook's hat and holding a skillet in one hand. The man figures it must be a messenger from the other side and yells to her: 'Do you know anything about parachutes?' The woman answers: 'No. You know anything about gas cookers?'

League table of sense of humour

We asked everyone participating in LaughLab to tell us which country they were from. We analysed the data from the ten countries that rated the highest number of jokes. The following league table lists the countries in the order of how funny they found the jokes:

Most funny

Germany

France

Denmark

UK

Australia

The Republic of Ireland

Belgium

USA

New Zealand

Canada

Least funny

Does this mean that Germans have the best sense of humour? Or is there perhaps very little to laugh at in Germany, so any jokes are seen as very funny? Or perhaps it's all due to another factor completely. Perhaps it is all about happiness . . .

We asked people taking part in LaughLab to rate how happy they felt before rating the jokes. The results showed an interesting connection with the previous list, with Germany topping the league again:

Most happy

Germany
UK
France
Australia
Belgium
Denmark
USA
Canada
New Zealand
The Republic of Ireland

Least happy

So, perhaps Germans rated the jokes as funniest because they were the happiest participants.

Most frequently submitted joke

What's brown and sticky?
A stick.

This joke was submitted to LaughLab over 300 times.

And no-one ever found it very funny.

Joke Score = 2%.

 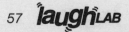

LaughLab's most contrived joke

We saw lots of contrived jokes, but none more so than the following:

Three friends travel to Canada's north to hunt black bears. They include a Czechoslovakian, a Frenchman and an Englishman. Their guide drops them off in the wilderness and tells them he will return the following week to pick them up.

A week later, the guide returns to the drop-off spot to find the camp deserted. After an hour of searching he calls in the Royal Canadian Mounted Police to conduct a search. After several hours, they come upon two large, black bears covered with blood. Of course, everyone comes to the same conclusion – the three guys were killed by the bears, one a male and the other a female bear.

One officer takes aim and shoots both bears dead. To find out exactly what happened, the officer takes out his large knife, cuts open the female bear's belly and finds the remains of the Frenchman and Englishman.

He looks up and says: 'I guess the Czech's in the male.'

*Wit ought to be a glorious treat like caviar;
never spread it around like marmalade.*

NOËL COWARD

Top surreal jokes

Surrealism figured strongly in some of the LaughLab submissions. Here are the top five surreal jokes:

 What do you do with a wombat?
Play wom.

 What is grey?
A melted penguin.

 An elephant and a mouse were talking together. The elephant said to the mouse: 'Why am I so big and strong and heavy and you are so tiny, weak and puny and grey?'
The mouse said: 'Well, I've been ill haven't I!'

 A baby polar bear goes to its mother and asks: 'Mummy, am I a polar bear?' 'Why, yes!' she replies. 'So, I'm not a grizzly bear, then.'
'No darling.'
The baby goes to its father and says: 'Daddy, am I really a polar bear? Might I be a koala bear, or a black bear instead?'
Daddy bear says: 'NO! You're a polar bear, just like your mother and father. Why are you asking these questions?'
The baby bear replies: 'Because I'm bloody freezing!'

And the winning surreal joke is:

An Alsatian went to a telegram office, took out a blank form and wrote: 'Woof. Woof. Woof. Woof. Woof. Woof. Woof. Woof. Woof.'
The clerk examined the paper and politely told the dog: 'There are only nine words here. You could send another 'Woof' for the same price.'
'But,' the dog replied, 'that would make no sense at all.'

laughLAB

LaughLab's strangest joke

We had many strange submissions to LaughLab, but the award for the strangest of the strange goes to the following:

> If a wheel falls off a bus while travelling down a river,
> how long will it take to shingle a dog house?
> None, because there's no bones in cottage cheese!

Joke Score = 16%

Answers on a postcard to . . .

Does length matter?

Just for fun, we had the LaughLab computer count the
number of words in every joke that people submitted.

> On average . . .
> . . . the jokes contained forty words.
> But . . .
> . . . the funniest jokes contained one hundred and three
> words.

It seems that if a joke is too short then people don't get
'into' it, too long and they lose interest.
   According to the data, one hundred and three words is
exactly right.

 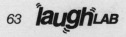

LaughLab's shortest joke

The shortest joke we received was just three words long:

Gargoyle: olive-flavoured mouthwash.

This obtained a Joke Score of just 6%.

LaughLab's longest joke

The longest submission to LaughLab was 339 words long:

A man walks up to the bar with an ostrich behind him. As he sits, the bartender comes over and asks for his order.

The man says: 'I'll have a beer.' and turns to the ostrich. 'What about you?'

'I'll have a beer, too,' says the ostrich. The bartender pours the beer and says: 'That will be $3.40 please.' and the man reaches into his pocket and pulls out exact change for payment.

The next day, the man and ostrich come again, and the man says: 'I'll have a beer.' and the ostrich says: 'I'll have the same.' Once again the man reaches into his pocket and pays with exact change. This becomes a routine until, late one evening, the two enter again.

'The usual?' asks the bartender.

'Well, it's close to last call, so I'll have a large scotch,' says the man. 'Same for me,' says the ostrich. 'That will be $7.20,' says the bartender.

Once again the man pulls the exact change out of his pocket and places it on the bar. The bartender can't hold back his curiosity any longer. 'Excuse me, sir. How do you manage to always come up with the exact change out of your pocket every time?'

'Well,' says the man, 'several years ago I was cleaning the attic and found an old lamp. When I rubbed it a Genie appeared and offered me two wishes. My first wish was that if I ever had to pay for anything, I just put my hand in my pocket, and the right amount of money will always be there.'

'That's brilliant!' says the bartender. 'Most people would wish for a million dollars or something, but you'll always be as rich as you want for as long as you live!' 'That's right! Whether it's a gallon of milk or a Rolls Royce, the exact money is always there,' says the man.

The bartender asks: 'One other thing, sir, what's with the ostrich?'

The man replies: 'My second wish was for a chick with long legs.'

This obtained a Joke Score of 39%.

How to spot a fake smile

There are huge differences between a genuine smile and a fake smile.

When people actually find a joke funny, the zygomatic muscles around their mouths pulls the corners of their lips upwards, and the obicularis oculi muscles around their eyes raise their cheeks and crinkle the corners of the eyes, creating lots of tiny 'crow's feet'.

A fake smile is quite different. When people pretend to find a joke funny, they only smile with their mouths and do not raise their cheeks, resulting in a lack of crinkling around the eyes.

A fake smile also lasts longer than the genuine one, and stops more abruptly.

So now you know how to discover whether or not people really find your jokes funny!

 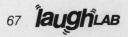

Best joke involving a Buddhist and a hot-dog vendor

Okay, so we made up the category, but we really liked the joke and wanted an excuse to include it:

> A Buddhist walks up to a hot dog vendor and says: 'Make me one with everything.'

This joke was submitted by Elisabeth, 24, from Tennessee in the USA:

I like it because it's short, but very subtle and clever.

So do we, Elisabeth.

It's the way I type them

People occasionally mistyped their jokes and managed to render them completely unfunny. Here is one of our favourite examples of this.

The joke should have been:

> How do you get two whales in a car?
> Go up the M4.

But someone typed it as:

> How do you fit two whales in a car?
> Go up the M4.

Both jokes were submitted to LaughLab. The Joke Score for the first joke was 26%, compared to just 2% for the second one.

 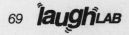

Monty Python and the world's funniest joke

The Monty Python team once produced a sketch based entirely around the idea of the world's funniest joke.

The sketch takes place in the 1940s. A man called Ernest Scribbler thinks of the world's funniest joke, writes it down, and then dies laughing. The joke is so funny that it kills anyone who reads it. Eventually, the British military realize that the joke could be used as a lethal weapon, and have a team of people translate it into German.

Each person translates just one word at a time in order not to be affected by the joke. The joke is then read out to German forces, and is so funny that they are unable to fight because they are laughing so much.

The joke helps the British win the war, and its use only comes to an end when joke warfare is banned at a special session of the Geneva Convention.

Variations on a theme

Sometimes, we also had the same joke submitted with different wordings. Interestingly, these subtle variations could make a big difference to the Joke Scores.

Take the following two jokes:

Joke A   A turtle was walking down an alley in New York when he was mugged by a gang of snails. A police detective came to investigate and asked the turtle if he could explain what happened. The turtle looked at the detective with a confused look on his face and replied: 'I don't know, it all happened so fast.'

Joke B   While sliding along through the forest one day, a snail was overturned by a gang of turtles. He lay under a bush, dazed, until another snail happened by and helped him up. 'What happened?' asked his rescuer. 'I don't know!' replied the snail, 'It all happened so fast!'

Joke B was rated as being much funnier than the first and thus it has been scientifically proven that turtles being attacked by snails is funnier than snails being attacked by turtles. So now you know.

GSOH

Professor Robert Provine, from the University of Maryland, once conducted a study into humour and personal ads.[9]
He studied 3,745 ads that had been placed in eight major American newspapers.

The percentage of women seeking men with a good sense of humour was over twice that of men seeking humorous women. Not only that, the ads revealed that there was a far greater percentage of men than women describing themselves as humorous.

Provine concluded that the message was clear: women seek men who make them laugh, and men are anxious to comply with this request.

Research shows that . . .

. . . children laugh about 400 times a day.[10]

. . . adults laugh on average about 18 times a day.[11]

Eskimos use the word 'laugh' to refer to lovemaking – to 'laugh with' someone is to have intercourse with them.

More variations on a theme

Joke A   After a long and fruitful life, Angus MacDonald died. His widow called the local paper, requesting that a death notice be published. Ever frugal, she asked that the notice simply state Angus dead. The newspaper representative told her that death notices must have a minimum of five words. 'Fine,' she said, 'make it "Angus dead; Volvo for sale".'

Joke B   A man died and his wife phoned the newspaper to place an obituary. She called the obituary department and said: 'This is what I want to print: "Bernie is dead".' The man at the newspaper said: 'But for $25 you are allowed to print six words.' The woman answered, 'OK. Then print: "Bernie is dead. Toyota for sale".'

Joke A was seen as much funnier than Joke B. Perhaps this was because Joke A evokes the (obviously false) stereotype that Scottish people are mean, or perhaps it is because Volvos are simply funnier than Toyotas.

Prejudice and stereotypes

People in almost every country in the world tell jokes in which a certain group of people look silly or stupid. The actual group being targeted varies from country to country.

Research shows that the following countries tend to make jokes at the expense of the following groups:[12]

Britain	⟶	Irish
America	⟶	Polish
Canada	⟶	Newfies
France	⟶	Belgians
Germany	⟶	Ostfriedlanders

Interestingly, the Scots are seen as the most 'canny' right across the world, including in the UK, France, Canada, Sweden, Greece, Australia, South Africa and New Zealand.

 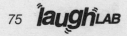

When was copper wire invented?
When two Scotsmen came across a penny in the street.

Joke Score by people in Scotland = 15%.
Joke Score by people in England = 27%.

Why don't English rugby players get vaccinated before touring?
They never catch anything.

Joke Score by people in Scotland = 25%.
Joke Score by people in England = 15%.

Top 'idiot' jokes

We received hundreds of jokes involving different groups of people appearing to be idiotic. To avoid any possible offence, we often replaced the particular group being targeted with the word 'idiot'. Here are the top four 'idiot' jokes:

 An idiot telephones his friend and says: 'Hello? Look, I bought a jigsaw puzzle but I can do it! I really can do it!'
His friend arrives at the house, takes one look at the situation and says: 'OK, this is what we will do – you put all the cornflakes back in the box and we won't ever talk about this again.'

 What do you do if an idiot throws a grenade at you? Take the pin out and throw it back!

 An idiot was walking along a river, when he spied another idiot on the other side. The first idiot yelled to the second idiot: 'HOW DO I GET TO THE OTHER SIDE?'
The second idiot responded immediately: 'YOU'RE ALREADY <u>ON</u> THE OTHER SIDE!'

 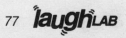

And the winning 'idiot' joke is:

An idiot really wanted to go ice fishing. He'd seen many books on the subject and, after getting all the necessary tools, he made for the nearest frozen lake. After positioning his footstool, he started to make a circular cut in the ice. Suddenly – from the sky – a voice boomed: 'THERE ARE NO FISH UNDER THE ICE!' Startled, the idiot moved further down the ice, and began to cut yet another hole. Again, from the heavens, the voice bellowed: 'THERE ARE NO FISH UNDER THE ICE!' The idiot, now quite worried, moved way down to the opposite end of the ice, set up his stool, and tried again to cut his hole. The voice came once more, even louder: 'THERE ARE NO FISH UNDER THE ICE!'

He stopped, looked skyward, and said: 'Is that you, Lord?'

The voice replied: 'NO, THIS IS THE ICE RINK MANAGER! THERE ARE NO FISH UNDER THE ICE!'

How do you keep an idiot in suspense?
I'll tell you later . . .

The importance of not being too Ernest

Researchers have discovered that people who routinely use humour to cope with the problems in their lives are generally less anxious and stressed than others.[13] As comedian Bill Cosby once remarked: 'If you can laugh at it, you can survive it.'

Laughter also increases our general psychological well-being. People who laugh more are much happier, and more satisfied with their lives, than others.[14]

In fact, psychologists have shown that one of the most successful ways of increasing people's life satisfaction is to simply have them watch good comedy films. This is more effective than giving them a small gift, having them say the phrase, 'I really do feel good' over and over again, and having them listen to cheerful music.[15]

And years of laboratory research have uncovered that films involving John Cleese and Peter Sellers are especially good at making people laugh and feel better about themselves and their lives.

Bonding

Laughter helps us bond with each other because it sends out a powerful signal that we like being around people and that people enjoy being around us.

Research has shown that:

 people who laugh more tend to be liked more by their friends.[16]

 teachers who use humour are liked more by their pupils.[17]

 groups of employees who laugh together are more productive than those who are more serious.[18]

★ employees enjoy their jobs more when their supervisors have a good sense of humour.[19]

The effects of laughter extend far beyond friendship and the workplace. People who laugh more are seen as more attractive and tend to form more intimate relationships with others.[20] In short, laughter can be good for your love life, too!

 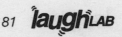

Comedian and musician Victor Borge once described humour as the shortest distance between two people.

Do animals laugh?

Contrary to popular belief, hyenas don't laugh. When excited, especially when being attacked by another hyena, some hyenas make a giggling noise, but this is more like a bark than a laugh.

However, Darwin noticed that both chimpanzees and orang-utans make a laugh-like sound when tickled, and primate experts Dian Fossey and Jane Goodall have described how gorillas chuckle when they tickle one another. Other researchers have found that lightly stroking rats can cause them to emit ultrasonic vocalisations that may be the rat equivalent of the human laugh.[21]

Over 2,000 years ago, Aristotle speculated that humans are the only creatures that laugh. It seems that he may well have been correct – although some animals laugh when tickled, many scientists believe only humans laugh in response to 'funny' situations and jokes.

Animal crackers

Early on in LaughLab, we had the following submission:

> There were two cows in a field. One said: 'Moo.' The
> other one said: 'I was going to say that!'

We decided to use the joke as a basis for a mini LaughLab experiment. We re-entered the joke into LaughLab several times, but used a different animal and animal noise each time.

At the end of the study we examined how the different animals had affected how funny people found the joke. This allowed us to discover the world's funniest animal.

Here are the results . . .

The league of funny animals

 Two tigers are walking through the jungle. One turns to the other and says: 'Gruurrr.' The other says: 'I was going to say that.'

 Two birds are perched in a tree. One turns to the other and says: 'Cheep Cheep.' The other says: 'I was going to say that.'

 Two mice are sitting in a field. One turns to the other and says: 'Eeeck Eeeck.' The other says: 'I was going to say that.'

 Two salamanders are sitting in a place where salamanders live. One turns to the other and makes a noise like a salamander. The other says: 'I was going to say that.'

 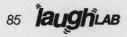

Funny animals continued

Two dogs are sitting in the street. One turns to the other and says: 'Woof.' The other says: 'I was going to say that.'

Two lions are walking through the jungle. One turns to the other and says: 'Roar.' The other says: 'I was going to say that.'

There were two cows in a field. One said: 'Moo.' The other one said: 'I was going to say that!'

Two cats are sitting in a garden. One turns to the other and says: 'Meow.' The other says: 'I was going to say that.'

And the winning funny animal was . . .

Two ducks were sitting in a pond, one of the ducks
said: 'Quack.' The other duck said: 'I was going to
say that!'

And so it's official: ducks are the funniest animals. Perhaps
it's because of their beaks, or webbed feet, or odd shape?

Regardless, the implication is clear – if you are going to
tell a joke involving an animal, make it a duck.

 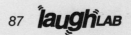

Clowns and comedians

There is a well-known story in which a man goes to see a doctor because he's feeling very sad. Rather than prescribe him any medication, the doctor recommends that he goes to see a performance by a famous clown called Grock. The doctor says: 'Grock is a very funny man and will soon have you laughing and feeling much better.'

The man looks at the doctor and replies: 'But you don't understand, I am Grock.'

And Grock is not the only unhappy clown. In fact, many comedians report feeling sad and lonely. One survey revealed that 85% of male comedians have sought some form of psychotherapy at some point in their lives.[22] And some of the world's most famous comedians, such as Tony Hancock, Lenny Bruce and John Belushi, are believed to have committed suicide.

Perhaps it is the stresses and strains of constantly having to be funny, or perhaps comedians have a tendency to suffer from low self-esteem. In either case, it is clear that having to be funny all of the time is often a very serious business.

W.C. Fields once explained why he felt drawn to comedy:

*'...the pleasure that I cause them
tells me that, at least for a short moment,
they love me.'*

*'...the only thing that matters
is making little jokes.'*

EDWARD LEAR

'There's a weasel chomping on my privates'

Dave Barry is a well-known humorist whose columns are syndicated in many American newspapers. In January 2002 he kindly devoted an entire column to LaughLab. At the end of the column he urged readers to submit jokes that simply ended with the punch line:

'There's a weasel chomping on my privates.'

Within just a few days we had received over 1,500 'weasel chomping' jokes. Here are some of the best, along with their ratings.

Weasel jokes

8 A guy walks into a bar and sits down. It takes him a few minutes to get the bartender's attention, because he keeps glancing at a ragged-looking older man and a beautiful young woman a few stools down. Finally the bartender comes down and asks him what he'd like.

'Well, I'd like a little bit quicker service next time,' the man says.

'Oh, really?' says the bartender.

'Yeah,' says the guy. 'Why were you paying so much attention to the two of them?'

The bartender responded: 'Because there's a weasel chomping on their privates.'

7 Why did the chicken cross the road?
Because a weasel was chomping on his privates.

This was submitted over 250 times!

 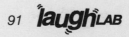

6 Tony Blair called George W. Bush to discuss international measures against biological warfare. 'Mr President,' Blair said. 'I believe the most effective precaution would be to install biological weapons detectors in every airport, train station and bus station.' George W. Bush was silent. 'Would you agree, Mr President?' Blair asked. Silence. 'Mr President, are you there?'
'Yeah, Tone, I'm here,' Bush finally said.
Tony Blair asked him why he hadn't said anything the whole time.
'I would have spoken up sooner,' Bush answered. 'But there was a WEASEL chomping on my PRIVATES!'

5 Why do elephants have big ears?
Because there's a weasel chomping on their privates.

Two baboons – an alpha male and a submissive female – are walking through the forest. Charlie, the alpha male, starts flirting and beating his chest to get the attention of Carol, the female. She accepts his come on and invites him to mate. Suddenly he blurts out: 'I can't do this' and she says: 'But you beat your chest so hard!'
Charlie replies: 'That may be, but there is a weasel chomping on my privates!'

 What makes buffaloes upset?
When there's a weasel chomping on their privates.

 Knock knock.
Who's there?
Theresa.
Theresa who?
Theresa weasel chomping on my privates!

 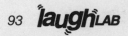

And the top 'weasel' joke is . . .

At the parade, the colonel noticed something unusual going on and asked the major: 'Major Barry, what the devil's wrong with Sergeant Jones' platoon? They seem to be all twitching and jumping about.'
'Well, sir,' says Major Barry after a moment of observation. 'There seems to be a weasel chomping on his privates.'

As we will see later on in the book, this joke cropped up again and again throughout our research.

The 'Got any nails?' joke

We received lots of variations of a joke in which an animal goes into a shop and is threatened with having part of its anatomy nailed to an object. Four were considered enough to illustrate the case:

4 A duck walks into a drugstore, and asks the cashier if he has any beer. The man says: 'No, this is a Drugstore, we don't sell beer here.' The Duck leaves, and returns home. The next day, he comes back to the store and asks the cashier again. The man replies: 'I told you yesterday! We don't sell beer here! If you ask me one more time, I am going to nail your feet to the floor!' The duck leaves again. One final time the duck enters the store the next day, and this time says: 'Do you have any nails?'
The man replies: 'No.'
The duck then says: 'Do you have any beer?'

A rabbit went into a butcher's shop and said: 'Got any carrots?'

The butcher said: 'No!'

The rabbit went back to the butchers the next day and said: 'Got any carrots?'

The butcher said: 'No!'

The rabbit went back the next day and said: 'Got any carrots?'

The butcher said: 'No! And if you come back tomorrow and ask if I have any carrots I'll nail your ears to the ceiling!'

The rabbit went back to the butchers the next day and asked: 'Got any nails?'

The butcher said: 'No!'

The rabbit said: 'In that case, have you got any carrots?'

 A penguin walks into a store and asks the teller: 'Do you have any grapes?'

'No,' he replies. This same thing happens the next day. On the third day the teller replies: 'No, and if you come in asking for grapes again, I will nail your flippers to the floor!'

The next day the penguin walks in and asks: 'Got any nails?' 'No,' replies the teller.

'Got any grapes?' the penguin asks.

And the winning 'Got any nails?' joke is:

A duck walks into a post office and asks the postman: 'Do you have any corn?' The postman answers politely: 'No, we don't have any corn here.' The next day the duck enters the store again and asks: 'Do you have any corn?'

A bit annoyed the postman answers: 'No! We don't have any corn.'

This goes on for a couple of days. Finally one day when the duck asks: 'Do you have any corn?', the postman gets so upset he yells: 'NO! For the last time, we don't have any corn, and if you ask again, I'll nail your beak to the counter!'

The next day the duck returns to the store and asks: 'Do you have any nails?'

The postman answers: 'No.'

Then the duck asks: 'Do you have any corn?'

So, we had four variations:

★ A duck asking for beer and having its feet nailed to the floor.

★ A rabbit asking for carrots and having its ears nailed to the ceiling.

★ A penguin asking for grapes and having its flippers nailed to the floor.

★ A duck asking for corn and having its beak nailed to the counter.

In case anyone ever asks you, our data showed that when it comes to the 'Got any nails?' joke, the duck/corn/beak combo is a clear winner.

More evidence, as if any were needed, that ducks are indeed the funniest animals.

Smile and (half) the world smiles with you

American researchers have examined the effect that our smiles have on other people.

They visited a shopping centre, and one experimenter either smiled or frowned at the people who walked past him, whilst another secretly observed whether the person reciprocated with a smile or a frown.

Nearly 40% of people responded to the experimenter's smile with another smile. In contrast, only 6% of them frowned when the experimenter frowned at them.

The researchers neatly summarised their findings in the title of their article: 'Smile, and (Half) the world smiles with you, frown and you frown alone'.[23]

Laughing epidemics

Laughing can be infectious and, like many other types of infection, has the potential to become an epidemic.

Perhaps the best-known example of a 'laughter plague' occurred in Tanganyika (now Tanzania)[24], where, in January 1962, three girls at a boarding school started laughing. Soon, the symptoms of laughter and agitation spread to 95 of the 159 pupils, and the school was forced to shut down for over two months. During this time, individual attacks of laughter lasted between a few minutes to a couple of hours. In some extreme cases these symptoms persisted for over two weeks.

The plague slowly spread to nearby villages over the course of the next two-and-a-half years, affecting over 1,000 people and resulting in the closure of over fourteen schools.

In the end, quarantining those infected with laughter proved the only way of controlling and ending the epidemic.

The Laughter Clubs of India

Dr Madan Kataria is the founding father of India's Laughter Clubs.[25]

Members of these clubs usually meet in public parks and simply laugh. The process is simple: One or two experienced members of the group start off by laughing. The effects are contagious and quickly spread to other members of the group. Soon everyone is engaged in full-on, hearty laughter.

Kataria formed his original group in Bombay in 1995. Since then over one hundred groups have sprung up all over India. According to its practitioners, Laughter Clubs help people lower their inhibitions, boost their self-confidence, help their breathing, and alleviate hypertension, arthritis and migraines.

In 1998, over 10,000 people attended a 'World Laughter Day' at the Bombay Racetrack. 'We all had a jolly good laugh,' said Kataria.

Laugh tracks

Because laughter is contagious, many television comedy shows include a 'laugh track' to encourage viewers to laugh.[26]

The first laugh track was used on 9 September 1950, on an American comedy show called *The Hank McCune Show*.

The technology behind modern-day laugh tracks was pioneered by engineer Charlie Douglas.

According to Jay Sommers, creator/producer of the American comedy show *Green Acres*: 'People are so conditioned to the laugh track that if they don't hear it they don't know it's a comedy show.'

Comedy is all about timing

Our computers recorded the time (Greenwich Mean Time) that each person rated the jokes in LaughLab. At the end of the experiment, we looked at the data from people who had logged on from the UK and examined how the degree to which they found jokes funny changed over the course of the day.

The graph is shown below:

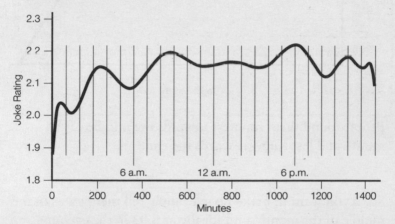

It reveals that:

> People found the jokes funniest at 6.03 in the evening.

> People found them least funny at 1.30 in the morning.

So, if you want to make people laugh, tell them the joke at 6.03 p.m.

 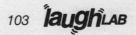

Best time of the month to tell a joke

We also recorded the date that each person visited LaughLab. There were huge differences in how funny people found jokes at different times during the month.

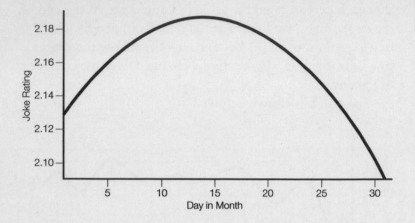

People found them funniest towards the middle of the month and less funny towards the end.

So, if you want to make people laugh, tell them jokes in the middle of the month, and ideally at 6.03 in the evening.

Impact of the weather

With the help of the Met Office, we were able to examine whether we find jokes funnier when the sun shines.

We looked at the relationship between the amount of sunshine in the UK in any one week, and the degree to which people in the UK found the LaughLab jokes funny during that week.

There was a clear relationship – sunshine puts a smile on our faces, makes us feel good and more likely to laugh at jokes.

 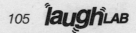

Best day of the year to tell a joke

Careful analysis of the data revealed that people found the jokes funniest on 7 October.

We therefore confidently predict that 6.03 p.m. on the 7 October each year will be a hilarious moment.

Especially if it happens to be sunny.

three top tickle theories

So now we have seen some of the winning jokes from LaughLab. But why do these jokes bring a smile to our faces whilst others make us groan? To find out, it is time to travel backstage and examine the theory behind the laughter.

A serious work in philosophy could be written entirely of jokes.

LUDWIG WITTGENSTEIN

Theory One – Superiority

Why do people tend to laugh when someone slips over a banana skin or has a custard pie slapped into their face?

Well, according to one theory of humour, we laugh because these types of situations make us feel superior to other people. The person who tripped over the banana skin, or was the recipient of the custard pie, has been made to look silly and that makes us feel good. In fact, it makes us feel so good that we laugh.

The superiority theory also explains why we laugh at certain types of jokes. Many jokes make us feel superior to other people. In these types of jokes, people appear stupid because they have misunderstood an obvious situation, made a stupid mistake, been the hapless victim of unfortunate circumstance or have been made to look stupid by someone else. According to the theory, these jokes cause us to laugh because they make us feel superior to other people.

 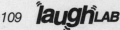

Superiority Jokes

Here are a few 'superiority' jokes from LaughLab:

> A woman goes into a cafe with a duck. She puts the duck on a stool and sits next to it.
> The waiter comes over and says: 'Hey! That's the ugliest pig that I have ever seen.'
> The woman says: 'It's a duck, not a pig.'
> And the waiter says: 'I was talking to the duck.'

> Texan: 'Where are you from?'
> Harvard grad: 'I come from a place where we do not end our sentences with prepositions.'
> Texan: 'OK – where are you from, jackass?'

Scientists and philosophers have been studying humour for over 2,000 years. The famous philosopher, Plato (427–348 BC), was one of the first people to advance the 'superiority' theory. But he was not a fan of laughter. He thought that it was wrong to laugh at the misfortune of others and that hearty laughter involved a loss of control that resulted in people appearing to be less than fully human.

As a result, he urged people to refrain from laughing.

A man was walking in the countryside and came across a shepherd and a large flock of sheep. He says to the shepherd: 'I bet you £50 against one of your sheep that I can tell you the exact number in this flock.'

The shepherd thinks it over; it's a big flock so he takes the bet.

'145,' says the man.

The shepherd is astonished, because that is exactly right. He says: 'OK, I'm a man of my word, take an animal.' The man picks one up and begins to walk away. 'Wait,' cries the shepherd. 'let me have a chance to get even. Double or nothing that I can guess your exact occupation.' The man agrees. 'You are a policy adviser for the Ministry of Agriculture,' says the shepherd.

'Amazing!' responds the man. 'You are exactly right! But tell me, how did you deduce that?'

'Well,' says the shepherd, 'put down my dog and I will tell you.'

Theory Two – Freud on fun

Sigmund Freud was one of the most influential thinkers of the twentieth century.

His basic idea was that we all have sexual and aggressive thoughts, but that society does not allow us to express these ideas openly. As a result, they become repressed deep into our unconscious and only emerge via the odd slip of the tongue (the 'Freudian slip') in dreams and certain forms of psychotherapy.

But Freud was also fascinated by jokes and humour. He believed that they represented another way in which people could release their pent-up thoughts in a socially acceptable way. Thoughts about death, sex, marriage, authority figures, certain bodily functions, anything, in fact, that it is socially unacceptable to say with a straight face.

So, to Freud, humour provides a kind of relief – a way of coping with the problems in our lives, or issues that we are embarrassed or reluctant to confront.

Freudian Funnies

Although many of the jokes submitted to LaughLab fit with Freud's ideas, they didn't make it through our vetting procedure because they weren't suitable for family viewing. However, here are some examples that fit the theory and did get the green light:

A patient says: 'Doctor, last night I made a Freudian slip, I was having dinner with my mother-in-law and wanted to say: "Could you please pass the butter." But instead I said: "You silly cow, you have completely ruined my life".'

A woman told her friend: 'For eighteen years my husband and I were the happiest people in the world! Then we met.'

A newly ordained priest is nervous about hearing confessions and asks an older priest to observe one of his sessions to give him some tips. After a few minutes of listening, the old priest suggests that they have a word. 'I've got a few suggestions,' he says. 'Try folding your arms over your chest and rub your chin with one hand.' The new priest tries this. 'Very good,' says his senior. 'Now try saying things like "I see", "I understand" and "Yes, go on".' The younger priest practises these sayings, too. 'Well done,' says the older priest. 'Don't you think that's better than slapping your knee and saying: "No way! What happened next?"'

 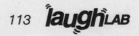

An 8-year-old girl went to her dad, who was working in the yard.

She asked him: 'Daddy, what is sex?'

The father was surprised that she would ask such a question, but decided that if she was old enough to ask the question, then she was old enough to get a straight answer. He proceeded to tell her all about the 'birds and the bees'. When he finished explaining, the little girl was looking at him with her mouth hanging open. The father asked her: 'Why did you ask this question?'

The little girl replied: 'Mum told me to tell you that dinner would be ready in just a couple of secs.'

Theory Three – Incongruity

The most popular theory of why we find jokes funny revolves around the concept of 'incongruity'. One of the first people to discuss the incongruity theory of jokes in any great detail was the famous eighteenth-century German philosopher, Immanuel Kant. The idea is that we laugh at things that surprise us because they seem out of place. For example, it's funny when clowns wear outrageously large shoes, people have especially big noses or politicians tell the truth. In the same way, many jokes are funny because they involve ideas that run against our expectations. A bear walks into a bar. Animals talk. And so on.

But there is more to this theory than such simple forms of incongruity. In many jokes, there is an apparent incongruity between the set-up and the punch line.

Take the following joke:

> Two fish in a tank.
> One turns to the other and says: 'Do you know how to drive this?'

The set-up line leads us to think about two fish in a fish tank. But the punch line surprises us – why should the fish be able to drive a fish tank? Then, a split second later, we suddenly realise that the word 'tank' has two meanings, and that the fish are actually in an army tank. Scientists refer to this as the 'incongruity-resolution' theory. We resolve the incongruity caused by the punch line, and the accompanying feeling of sudden surprise makes us laugh.

 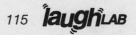

Sometimes, these sorts of jokes are very simple and consist of little more than puns. Other times they can be very complicated, and involve complex word plays or require us to look at people and situations in quite different ways.

Incongruous humour

The following LaughLab jokes illustrate different kinds of incongruity:

Did you hear about the man who drowned in a bowl of muesli?
He was pulled under by a strong currant!

So I went down to the local gym. I said: 'Can you teach me how to do the splits?'
He said: 'How flexible are you?'
I said: 'I can't make Tuesdays.'

Two owls are playing in the final of the Owl Pool Championship. It comes down to the last frame. One of the owls is just about to play his shot, when his wing accidentally touches a ball.
'That's two hits,' says the other owl.
'Two hits to who?' says the first.

Three budgies in a cage, one on the top perch, one on the middle and one on the bottom perch. Which budgie owns the cage?
The one on the bottom perch, the other two are on higher perches.

Did you hear about the ice-cream man who was found dead in his ice-cream van, covered in chocolate sauce and hundreds-and-thousands? The police said that he had topped himself.

Two aerials met on a roof, fell in love and got married. The ceremony was rubbish but the reception was brilliant.

 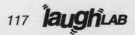

Continued incongruity

Riding the favourite at Cheltenham, a jockey was well ahead of the field. Suddenly he was hit on the head by a turkey and a string of sausages. He managed to keep control of his mount and pulled back into the lead, only to be struck by a box of Christmas crackers, a can of spam and a dozen mince pies as he went over the last fence. With great skill he managed to steer the horse to the front of the field once more when, on the run in, he was struck on the head by a bottle of sherry and a Christmas pudding. Thus distracted, he managed only a second placing. He immediately went to the stewards to complain that he had been seriously hampered.

So I was in my car, and I was driving along, and my boss rang up, and he said: 'You've been promoted.' And I swerved. And then he rang up a second time and said: 'You've been promoted again.' And I swerved again. He rang up a third time and said: 'You're managing director.' And I went into a tree. And a policeman came up and said: 'What happened to you?' And I said: 'I careered off the road.'

Patient: 'Doctor, I've got a strawberry stuck up my bum.'
Doctor: 'I've got some cream for that.'

 118

*Jokes join up the invisible dots
between two subjects.*

MEL CALMAN

 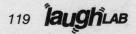

Brain research and incongruity

Have a look at the following set-up line and then the three possible punch lines, and see of you can choose the correct punch line.

Set-up line:

A man went up to a lady in a crowded square.
'Excuse me,' he said. 'Do you happen to have seen a policeman anywhere around here?'
'I'm sorry,' the woman answered, 'but I haven't seen one for ages.'

Potential punch lines:

A 'Oh, OK, can you give me your watch and necklace then.'
B 'Oh, OK, its just that I have been looking for one for half an hour.'
C 'Baseball is my favourite sport.'

The first punch line is obviously correct. The second one makes sense, but isn't funny. And the third does not make sense and isn't funny.

The amazing fact is that researchers have discovered that people with damage to the right side of the brain tended to choose the third punch line far more often than people who did not have any brain damage. It seems that these people know that the end of the joke should be surprising, but have no way of knowing that one of the punch lines could be reinterpreted to make sense, whilst the other could not.[27] Interestingly, these people still find films of slapstick comedians funny – they haven't lost their sense of humour, but rather have lost the ability to work out why certain incongruities are funny and others are not.

section three *further complex analyses*

In LaughLab we discovered that many of these theories helped explain why different groups of people have very different senses of humour: why men and women laugh at different jokes, why people from different countries find different jokes funny, and why our sense of humour changes as we get older.

The Battle of the Sexes

A husband stepped on one of those penny scales that tell you your fortune and weight, and dropped in a coin. 'Listen to this,' he said to his wife, showing her a small, white card. 'It says I'm energetic, bright, resourceful and a great person.' 'Yeah,' his wife nodded, 'and it has your weight wrong, too.'

A woman accompanied her husband to the doctor's office for a checkup. Afterwards, the doctor took the wife aside and said: 'Unless you do the following things, your husband will surely die.' The doctor went on to say: 'Here is what you need to do. Every morning make sure that you serve him a good healthful breakfast. Meet him at home each day for lunch, so that you can serve him a well-balanced meal. Make sure you serve him a good, hot meal each evening and do not overburden him with any stressful conversation, nor ask him to perform any household chores. Also, keep the house clean and spotless, so that he does not get exposed to any threatening germs.'
On the way home, the husband asked his wife what the doctor said.
She replied: 'You are going to die.'

Women thought that these jokes were very funny. Men didn't agree. The reason is all due to superiority. These jokes make women look good and put down men, and so they appeal far more to females than males.

Further appeals to female supremacy

A man left work one Friday afternoon. But, instead of going home, he stayed out the entire weekend hunting with the boys and spending his entire paycheque. When he finally got home on Sunday night, he was confronted by his very angry wife and was barraged for two hours. Finally, his wife stopped nagging and simply said to him: 'How would you like it if you didn't see me for two or three days?' To which he replied: 'That would be fine with me.'
Monday went by and he didn't see his wife, Tuesday and Wednesday came and went with the same results. Thursday the swelling went down just enough so he could see her a little out of the corner of his left eye.

A woman and her husband interrupted their vacation to go to the dentist. The woman said: 'I want a tooth pulled, and I don't want any pain killers because I'm in a big hurry.' She continued: 'Just extract the tooth as quickly as possible, and we'll be on our way.'
The dentist was quite impressed. 'You're certainly a courageous woman,' he said. 'Which tooth is it?'
The woman turned to her husband and said: 'Show him your tooth, dear.'

And it doesn't stop there . . .

A couple in their sixties are walking along the beach to admire the sunset. The wife sees a dirty lamp and the husband stoops down to dust it off. Magically, a genie appears out of nowhere and thanks the couple profusely for freeing him from his imprisonment. 'As a reward,' the genie says, 'I'll grant you each one wish.' The wife says: 'I want to sail around the world. Send me and my husband on a first-class luxurious cruise.' *POOF* She's suddenly holding two tickets on the finest ship around the world.

The genie turns to the husband: 'And for you, sir?' The husband looks at his wife, and leans in close to the genie: 'I want a wife that is thirty years younger than me.' *POOF* And he's suddenly ninety years old.

A priest conducts a service in a church. 'The person who puts the most in the church collection box can choose three hymns,' he says. The collection box comes back to him after being filled up and he finds that someone has donated a thousand pounds. 'Who has donated a thousand pounds?' he asks. A woman raises her hand. The priest invites her to the front and tells her to choose three hymns. Pointing at the three most handsome men in the church she says: 'I'll have him, him and him.'

You can't have it all your own way

A man goes into a shop to buy a Barbie doll for his daughter. The salesman says: 'Here we have "Barbie on the Beach" for $20, "Barbie at the Stable" for $20, "Barbie in the Kitchen" for $20, "Barbie Skiing" for $20 and this is our Super Special: "Barbie Divorced" for $180.'
'So why is that $180 when the others only cost $20?' asks the man.
'Well, it comes with Ken's house, Ken's car, Ken's boat and Ken's horse!'

'This day holds a lot of meaning for me. It was on this day two years ago that I lost my dear wife and children. I'll never forget that game of cards . . .'

These were rated as being very funny by men, but they didn't raise a titter among women. And, once again, this can be explained by the superiority theory – these jokes make men look good at women's expense, so they appeal far more to men than women.

Also in the men's department . . .

A worried man goes to see his priest. 'Father, I am worried. I think that my wife is trying to poison me.' Said the priest: 'Hold on my son, let me talk to your wife and come back to see me tomorrow, then I shall be able to give you some advice.' The following day, the priest arranged to visit the man and told him: 'Well my son, I have talked to your wife for nearly two hours. My advice to you is, take the poison.'

A man driving on a highway is pulled over by a police officer. The officer asks: 'Did you know your wife and children fell out of your car a kilometre back?' A smile creeps on to the man's face and he exclaims: 'Thank God! I thought I was going deaf!'

Two drunks are sitting at a bar. The first one says: 'What's this thing that they call a 'Breathalyzer'?' The second guy says: 'It's a bag that can tell how much you drank.' The first guy says: 'I married one of those things years ago.'

An elderly couple were on a cruise and it was really stormy. They were standing on the back of the boat watching the moon, when a wave came up and washed the old woman overboard. They searched for days and couldn't find her, so the captain sent the old man back to shore with the promise that he would notify him as soon as they found something. Three weeks went by and finally the old man got a fax from the boat. It read:

'Sir, sorry to inform you, we found your wife dead at the bottom of the ocean. We hauled her up to the deck and attached to her rear was an oyster and in it was a pearl worth $50,000 . . . please advise.'

The old man faxed back:

'Send me the pearl and re-bait the trap.'

All these made men guffaw and women groan.

But it's not just about superiority

A bloke said to me: 'I'm going to chop off the bottom of one of your trouser legs and put it in a library.'
I thought: 'That's a turn-up for the books.'

I've got a cat called Minton and when he eats shuttlecocks. I say 'bad Minton!!'

A man walks into a bar with a piece of tarmac under his arm. He says to the barman: 'A pint for me and one for the road.'

Did you hear about the young butcher who sat on a meat grinder?
He got a little behind in his orders!

What do Mexicans keep under the carpet?
Underlay! Underlay! Underlay!

What do all of these jokes have in common? Two things. First, they are seen as much funnier by women than men. Second, they are all good examples of complex word plays. Research has shown that women tend to be more linguistically skilled than men, and so tend to find jokes involving good word plays much funnier.

Superiority complex?

A man wakes up in hospital.
'Doctor, doctor, I can't feel my legs!'
'I know,' replies the doctor. 'We had to amputate your arms.'

A nun is waiting at a bus stop and a man comes stumbling out of a bar. He staggers up to the nun and starts punching her until she is on the ground, at which point he looks down at her and says: 'Not so tough now, are you Batman?'

Men found these jokes funny but women didn't. The reason is because they all involve aggression and are rather bleak. Men tend to find aggressive humour much funnier than women.

Men also liked these –
they're aggressive and nasty

While robbing a home, a burglar hears someone say: 'Jesus is watching you.' To his relief, he realises it is just a parrot mimicking something it had heard. The burglar asks the parrot: 'What's your name?'
The parrot says: 'Moses.'
The burglar goes on to ask: 'What kind of person names their parrot Moses?'
The parrot replies: 'The same kind of person that names his Rottweiler Jesus.'

What has two legs and bleeds profusely?
Half a cat.

How do you make a cat go 'woof'?
Pour petrol on it.

What do you call a monkey in a minefield?
A BABOOM!!!!!!!!!!

Of course, we had to discover the top jokes from a male and female perspective. And we think that you'll like one or the other.

 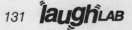

Top joke as voted by men

Two weasels are sitting on a bar stool. One starts to insult the other one.
He screams: 'I slept with your mother!'
The bar gets quiet as everyone listens to see what the other weasel will do. The first again yells: 'I SLEPT WITH YOUR MOTHER!'
The other says: 'Go home Dad, you're drunk.'

Top joke as voted by women

A man has six children and is very proud of his achievement. He is so proud of himself that he starts calling his wife 'Mother of Six', in spite of her objections. One night they go to a party. The man decides that it's time to go home, and wants to find out if his wife is ready to leave as well. He shouts at the top of his voice: 'Shall we go home Mother of Six?'

His wife, irritated by her husband's lack of discretion shouts back: 'Anytime you're ready, Father of Four!'

Nationality

People from many different countries participated in LaughLab. We analysed the data from the ten countries that rated the highest number of jokes, and discovered the following about how nationality influences our sense of humour . . .

An American approaches a British gentleman at a club, asks if he would like to play tennis.

The Brit replies: 'No, thank you, tried it once, didn't like it.'

The American asks if he would like to play billiards.

'No, thank you, tried it once, didn't like it.'

Would he like to play bridge?

'No, thank you, tried it once, didn't like it; but I see my son approaching. He might like to play.'

'Your only son I presume.'

Joke Score for the UK = 19%
Joke Score for the US = 45%

A Brit approaches an American at a club, and asks if he would like to play tennis.

The American replies, 'No, thank you, tried it once, didn't like it.'

The Brit asks if he would like to play billiards.

'No, thank you, tried it once, didn't like it.'

Would he like to play bridge?

'No, thank you, tried it once, didn't like it; but I see my son approaching. He might like to play.'

'Your only son I presume.'

Joke Score for the UK = 39%
Joke Score for the US = 14%

The conclusion, not surprisingly, is that people don't like jokes that put down people from their own country.

Another example

Farmer Fred has an American farmer visiting him. The American farmer is boasting about the size of his land in the United States: 'My land is so big, that it takes me two hours to drive around it by car.'
Farmer Fred is silent for a while. Then he nods and says: 'I know what you mean, once I had such a car, too.'

Europeans found this joke much funnier than Americans.

 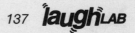

The ten countries fell into two groups, which we'll call Group A and Group B. They preferred quite different jokes.

Joke Set One

What's ET short for?
Because he's got little legs!

I saw this bloke chatting up a cheetah.
I thought: 'He's trying to pull a fast one'.

Two parrots sitting on a perch.
One says to the other: 'Can you smell fish?'

Two guys walk into a bar.
The third guy ducks.

These jokes were liked by Group A, but not Group B.

Joke Set Two

A man goes into a pet shop and says to the shop assistant: 'Can I have a pet wasp, please?'
The shop assistant replies: 'I'm sorry sir, we only sell normal pets here, like cats, dogs, budgies. We don't sell wasps.'
'Oh dear,' says the man. 'I thought I saw one in the window yesterday.'

Teacher: 'Dennis, if you had a dollar and you asked your mother for another dollar, how many dollars would you have?'
Dennis: 'One.'
Teacher: 'You don't know your arithmetic.'
Dennis: 'You don't know my mother.'

What do you call a sheep with no head or legs?
A cloud.

A man goes into an outfitters and asks: 'Do you sell camouflage jackets?'
'Yes,' replies the salesman. 'But we can't find them.'

These jokes were liked by Group B, but not Group A.

Given the type of jokes in each set, what do you think is the distinction?

The explanation is that Group A consisted of those countries that had English as their first language whilst Group B consisted of countries that didn't.

Group A – Countries that have English as their first language:

Australia
Canada
New Zealand
The Republic of Ireland
UK
US

Group B – Countries that do not have English as their first language:

Belgium
Denmark
France
Germany

The first set of jokes involves word puns that are difficult to 'understand' unless you have a very good grasp of the English language, and were therefore preferred by Group A. The second set of jokes are easy to understand, even if you do not have a very good grasp of the English language, and that's why they were preferred by Group B.

A further distinction

Why do elephants have big ears?
Because Noddy won't pay the ransom.

A farmer goes out one winter morning to find that all
his cows are frozen solid where they stand. While he
is wondering what to do, he sees a figure
approaching slowly across the fields. It is a little old
lady; she looks at the cows, then works her way
around the field, rubbing the nose of every cow in
turn. Slowly, each cow starts to warm up and come
back to life. The old lady rubs the nose of the last cow
and resumes her path across the fields.
The farmer stands amazed as his cows start to move
around again. At this moment his brother comes out
to see what is going on. The farmer explains what has
happened and points out the little old lady as she
disappears into the distance.
'Ah, well,' says the brother, 'you know who that is,
don't you? Thora Hird!'

Name two crustaceans.
King Crustacean & Charring Crustacean

These jokes worked in the UK but not elsewhere. Why?
Because they involve cultural references that only make
sense to people from the UK.

Top joke in the UK

A woman gets on a bus with her baby. The bus driver says: 'That's the ugliest baby that I've ever seen. Ugh!'
The woman goes to the rear of the bus and sits down, fuming. She says to a man next to her: 'The driver just insulted me!'
The man says: 'You go right up there and tell him off. Go ahead, I'll hold your monkey for you.'

This joke was submitted by Terry, 43, and his two daughters Catherine, 15, and Elizabeth, 11, from Vermont in the United States.

We all find this joke funny, although perhaps we differ as to exactly why. I laugh because I imagine what this baby might look like. My wife says it's because it could actually happen (my wife deceives herself, I think). My children think it's funny because monkeys are intrinsically funny. It has been a stock joke around our dinner table for some years now, and all we need to say is 'The Monkey Joke' to elicit a laugh.

Top joke in the US

At the parade, the Colonel noticed something unusual going on and asked the Major: 'Major Barry, what the devil's wrong with Sergeant Jones' platoon? They seem to be all twitching and jumping about.' 'Well, sir,' says Major Barry after a moment of observation. 'There seems to be a weasel chomping on his privates.'

Dave Barry strikes again!

And in second place:

A man and a friend are playing golf one day at their local golf course. One of the guys is about to chip on to the green when he sees a long funeral procession on the road next to the course. He stops in mid-swing, takes off his golf cap, closes his eyes, and bows down in prayer.
His friend says: 'Wow, that is the most thoughtful and touching thing I have ever seen. You truly are a kind man.'
The man then replies: 'Yeah, well we were married 35 years.'

The golfer joke was submitted by Mary Ruth, 40, from the Midwestern United States.

I heard the joke as a small child from my dad, who heard it from one of his golfing buddies. I like the joke for two reasons. I'm a devoted golfer myself and have been since a kid and enjoy golf jokes, especially ones that poke fun at putting golf ahead of everything else.

The second reason I like the joke I submitted is that it relies on the silly overstatement for its humor. Here in the states we tend to an overblown humor. It is really much the same as the so-called typical British humor that depends on the exaggerated understatement. Both take the normal to a funny extreme, whether over or understated.

Top joke in Canada

When NASA first started sending up astronauts, they quickly discovered that ballpoint pens would not work in zero gravity. To combat the problem, NASA scientists spent a decade and $12 billion to develop a pen that writes in zero gravity, upside down, underwater, on almost any surface including glass and at temperatures ranging from below freezing to 300°C. The Russians used a pencil.

Interestingly, the joke that most appealed to the Canadians involved putting down the Americans.

Top joke in France

A man visiting a farm notices a three-legged pig hobbling around. Thinking it strange such an animal should be kept on a working farm, he asked the farmer about it.

'Son,' said the farmer, 'that pig is a hero. There was a fire which started in the barn and had spread to the house while everybody was sleeping. That pig climbed out of its pen, and it freed all the other animals in the barn and led them to safety. Then that pig opened the back door to the house and got us all out before we had come to harm. Why, that pig saved the farm and the lives of my whole family.'

'Oh I see,' said the visitor. 'But why does the pig have only three legs?'

'Why son,' said the farmer, 'a pig like that you just don't eat all at once.'

The French went with a food-related joke as their top gag.

Top joke in Australia

This woman rushed to see her doctor, looking very much worried and all strung out. She rattles off: 'Doctor, take a look at me. When I woke up this morning, I looked at myself in the mirror and saw my hair all wiry and frazzled up, my skin was all wrinkled and pasty, my eyes were bloodshot and bugging out, and I had this corpse-like look on my face! What's WRONG with me, Doctor!?'
The doctor looks her over for a couple of minutes, then calmly says: 'Well, I can tell you that there ain't nothing wrong with your eyesight . . .'

 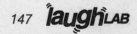

Top joke in Belgium

Why do ducks have webbed feet?
To stamp out fires.
Why do elephants have flat feet?
To stamp out burning ducks.

Oh dear.

Top joke in Denmark

Why do ducks have webbed feet?
To stamp out fires.
Why do elephants have flat feet?
To stamp out burning ducks.

Hummmm . . .

Top joke in New Zealand

At 3.30 a.m. a couple hear a knock at the door. The
man goes to answer and finds a man stood at his
doorstep. Having obviously been drinking the man
slurs: 'Would you mind giving me a push?'
The home owner apologises and says he needs to
get to sleep. He closes the door and returns to his
wife in bed. He tells his wife what the man wanted
and she says: 'Well aren't you going to help him?
Imagine if it was us stuck out there needing a hand
with the car!'
So the man goes downstairs and out of the door.
Because it was pitch black he shouts: ' Where are
you? I'll give you a push!'
To which he hears the reply: 'Great, I'm over here on
the swing!'

Top joke in the Republic of Ireland

Sean got home in the early hours of the morning after a night at the local pub. He made such a racket hitting into the furniture as he weaved his way through the house, that he woke up the missus.

'What on earth are you doing down there?' she yelled down from the bedroom. 'Get yourself up here to bed and don't waken the neighbours.'

'I'm trying to get a barrel of Guinness up the stairs,' he shouted.

'Leave it 'till the morning,' she shouted down.

'I can't,' he said. 'I've drank it!'

 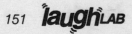

Top joke in Germany

There was a tie for the top joke in Germany between these two gags:

A general noticed one of his soldiers behaving oddly. The soldier would pick up any piece of paper he found, frown and say: 'That's not it.' and put it down again. This went on for some time, until the general arranged to have the soldier psychologically tested. The psychologist concluded that the soldier was deranged, and wrote out his discharge from the army. The soldier picked it up, smiled and said: 'That's it.'

Scientists have shown that the moon is moving away at a tiny, although measurable, distance from the Earth every year. If you do the maths, you can calculate that 85 million years ago the moon was orbiting the earth at a distance of about 35 feet from the Earth's surface. This would explain the death of the dinosaurs – the tallest ones, anyway.

Humour through the ages

Joke A   A boy is digging a hole in his back yard. The
neighbour asks why he's digging the hole.
The boy replies: 'My goldfish died. I have to bury
him.' The neighbour observes: 'That's a mighty
big hole for a goldfish.'
The boy says: 'Yeah, but he's in your cat.'

Joke B   What's the definition of a teenager?
God's punishment for enjoying sex.

Joke C   An old guy goes into confession and says to the
priest: 'Father, I'm 80 years old, married, have
four kids and eleven grandchildren, and last night
I had an affair, and I made love to two 18-year-
old girls. Both of them. Twice.'
The priest said: 'Well, my son, when was the last
time you were in confession?'
'Never Father, I'm Jewish.'
'So then, why are you telling me?'
'I'm telling everybody.'

Joke A was liked by children, Joke B by middle-aged people
and Joke C by older people. Why? Because people like
jokes that involve people of their own age looking good.
Once again, it evokes feelings of superiority. Joke A
involves a child putting down his adult neighbour, Joke B
puts down teenagers and in Joke C an old man boasts of
his achievements.

Joke A   In a 3rd grade class Johnny was asked if he knew what a cannibal was. He said to the teacher: 'No sir.'
'Well,' Johnny's teacher asked him, 'if you ate your parents what would you be?' Johnny replied: 'An orphan, sir.'

Joke B   A lawyer hired a young fellow to paint his porch, quite a large porch that wrapped around most of the house. He showed the painter several cans of paint and explained he would be working inside so the painter could inform him when the job was done. Half-an-hour later, the lawyer heard a knock on the door.
'I'm finished,' the painter told the astounded lawyer. 'I had plenty of paint, so I added a second coat.'
As the lawyer handed the painter the agreed-on payment, the painter remarked: 'Oh, by the way, it's a Ferrari, not a Porsche.'

Joke C   What is the difference between a doctor and God?
God doesn't think he is a doctor!

Once again, different age groups found certain jokes funnier than others. Children like Joke A, middle-aged people like Joke B and older people like Joke C. Why? Because they all involve laughing at authority figures that play an important role in these people's lives. Teachers have authority over children, lawyers over the middle-aged and doctors over the elderly.

Joke A Two kids were talking in the playground. The first kid says: 'My mum is from Ireland and my dad is from America. That makes me an Irish-American.'
The second kid says: 'Well, my mum is from Iceland and my dad is from Cuba. So I guess that makes me an Icecube.'

Joke B A dog called 'Rufus Jagger' walks into a bank. The teller says: 'Hello, my name is Sally Whack, how can I help you?'
The dog puts a keyring with a little toy elephant attached to it onto the counter and says: 'I'd like a loan please.'
Sally Whack, baffled by what's happening, picks up the keyring and calls her manager. She explains the situation and shows her manager the keyring.
The manager says: 'It's a nick nack Sally Whack, give the dog a loan, his old man's a rolling stone.'

Children like Joke A, whilst adults like Joke B. Perhaps not surprisingly, the types of incongruous word puns that appealed to people became more complicated as they became older.

More simple puns that appealed to children . . .

Customer: 'Waiter, this fish is bad.'
Waiter: 'You naughty fish, you!'

What do you get if you cross a snowman with a vampire?
Frostbite!

What is the difference between a golf player and a sky-diver?
The golfer goes: *Whack!* . . . 'Darn it!'
The sky diver goes: 'Darn it!' . . . *Whack!*

What you call a snowman with a suntan?
A puddle!

How do you get a skeleton to laugh?
Tickle its funny bone.

Some more complex puns that appealed to adults . . .

I had a clone made of myself . . . the problem was that he swore all the time. So I finally got mad and pushed him off a cliff . . . I was arrested. The police charged me with making an obscene clone fall.

Mahatma Gandhi, as you know, walked barefoot most of the time, which produced an impressive set of callouses on his feet. He also ate very little, which made him rather frail, and with his odd diet, he suffered from bad breath.
A super calloused fragile mystic hexed by halitosis.

A group of chess enthusiasts were kicked out of a hotel reception for discussing their winning games. The manager can't stand chess nuts boasting in an open foyer.

Did you hear about the Buddhist monk who refused to have his mouth frozen when he went to the dentist?
He wanted to transcend dental medication.

 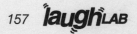

Duplication

Children like the sound of duplicated words – words that sound the same but are slightly different, like Humpty Dumpty. Perhaps the best example of this was the 'wonky donky' joke:

What do you call a donkey with one leg?
A wonky donkey.

What do you call a donkey with one leg and one eye?
A winky wonky donkey.

What do you call a donkey with one leg and one eye breaking wind?
A stinky winky wonky donkey.

What do you call a donkey with one leg and one eye breaking wind and wearing blue suede shoes?
A honky tonky stinky winky wonky donkey.

What do you call a donkey with one leg and one eye breaking wind, wearing blue suede shoes and playing a piano?
A plinky plonky honky tonky stinky winky wonky donkey.

What do you call a donkey with one leg and one eye breaking wind, wearing blue suede shoes, playing a piano and driving a bus?
Very talented.

It's who you know and what you know

Joke A Craig David, Shaggy and Britney Spears were
stuck in an elevator when they smelled
something like rotten eggs.
Craig David said: 'I'm walkin' away'.
Shaggy said: 'It wasn't me'.
And Britney Spears said: 'Oops I did it again.'

Joke B Where does Kylie get her kebabs from?
. . . Jason's Donervan!

Joke C How do you get pikachu on to a bus?
You pokemon.

Joke D What do you get when you play country music
backwards?
Your wife comes back, your dog's alive, you get
out of prison and it don't rain no more.

Children laughed at Jokes A, B, and C, whilst adults liked
Joke D. This is because to understand the incongruity in
Jokes A, B and C you have to understand something about
current pop music, whilst for Joke D you have to
understand something about Country and Western music.

The different age groups also tend to laugh most at jokes involving topics that concern and interest them.

Teenagers tend to find these jokes much funnier than adults . . .

Why do squirrels swim on their backs?
To keep their nuts dry.

A guy walked into a psychiatrist's office wearing only cling-film underpants. The psychiatrist said: 'Well, I can see you're nuts.'

A pirate walks into a bar with a steering wheel stuck in his pants. The bartender asks: 'Hey man isn't that annoying?'
The pirate says: 'Arrrrr, it's driving me nuts.'

The middle-aged enjoyed jokes about their relationships and mother-in-laws:

The other night I was invited out for a night with 'the boys'. I told my wife that I would be home by midnight . . . promise! Well, the hours passed and the beer was going down way too easy. At around 2:30 a.m., drunk as a skunk, I headed for home. Just as I got in the door, the cuckoo clock in the hall started up and cuckooed three times. Quickly, I realized she'd probably wake up, so I cuckooed another nine times. I was really proud of myself, having a quick-witted solution, even when smashed, to escape a possible conflict. The next morning my wife asked me what time I got in, and I told her twelve o'clock. She didn't seem disturbed at all. Whew! Got away with that one! She then told me that we needed a new cuckoo clock. When I asked her why, she said: 'Well, last night our clock cuckooed three times, then said 'oops,' cuckooed four more times, cleared its throat, cuckooed another three times, giggled, and cuckooed twice more.

 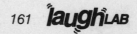

A man staggers into an emergency room with two black eyes and a golf club wrapped tightly around his throat. Naturally the doctor asks him what happened. 'Well, it was like this,' said the man. 'I married recently and I was making progress with establishing a relationship with my mother-in-law by having a pleasant round of golf. Then she sliced her ball into a pasture of cows. We went to look for it and while I was rooting around, I noticed one of the cows had something white at its rear end. I walked over and lifted up the tail and sure enough, there was my mother-in-law's golf ball stuck right in the middle of the cow's butt. That's when I made my mistake.'
'What did you do?' asks the doctor.
'Well, I lifted the tail and yelled, "Hey, this looks like yours!"'

And those in the older group often liked jokes about people's health:

A 90-year-old man goes to the doctor for a checkup. The doctor does a thorough examination and tells the man to return in six months for a follow-up exam. Six months later the old man returns. The doctor re-examines him and says: 'You are doing really well. Everything looks good.'
The old man replies: 'Well, Doctor, I just followed the advice you gave me the last time I was here.'
'What advice was that?' inquired the doctor.
'You told me to get a hot mama and be cheerful and that's just what I did,' the old man answered.
'That's not what I told you!' said the doctor. 'What I said was, you have a heart murmur. Be careful!'

A man in his late fifties suspects that his wife is going deaf, so he decides to test her hearing. He stands on the opposite side of the living room from her and asks: 'Can you hear me?' No answer. He moves halfway across the room toward her and asks: 'Can you hear me now?' No answer. He moves and stands right beside her and says: 'Can you hear me now?' She replies: 'For the third time, yes!'

 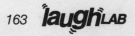

An elderly couple had dinner at another couple's house, and after eating, the wives left the table and went into the kitchen.

The two elderly gentlemen were talking, and one said: 'Last night, we went out to a new restaurant, and it was really great. I would recommend it very highly.'

The other man said: 'What was the name of the restaurant?'

The first man thought and thought and finally said: 'What is the name of that flower you give to someone you love? You know, the one that is red and has thorns.'

'Do you mean a rose?'

'Yes,' the man said. He then turned towards the kitchen and yelled: 'Rose, what's the name of that restaurant we went to last night?'

Top joke, as voted by people aged 11–15

A new teacher was trying to make use of her psychology courses. She started her class by saying: 'Everyone who thinks they're stupid, stand up!' After a few seconds, Little Johnny stood up.

The teacher said: 'Do you think you're stupid, Little Johnny?'

Little Johnny replied: 'No, ma'am, but I hate to see you standing there all by yourself.'

Top joke, as voted by people aged 30–40

A man makes it to the front of the supermarket check-out line. The check-out girl, while swiping through his frozen pizzas, TV dinners, case of beer, and TV guide, asks: 'You're single, aren't you?'

The man replies: 'Why, yes, I am single. How could you tell?'

'Well, because you're really ugly,' she answers.

Top joke, as voted by the over 50s

An elderly woman went to the police station with her next-door neighbour to report her husband was missing. The policeman asked for a description.
She said: 'He's 35 years old, 6 foot 4, has dark eyes, dark wavy hair, an athletic build, weighs 185 pounds, is soft-spoken, and is good to the children.'
The next-door neighbour protested: 'Your husband is 5 foot 4 inches, chubby, bald, has a big mouth, and is mean to your children.'
The wife replied: 'Yeah, but who wants HIM back?'

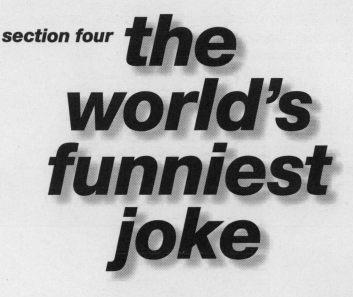

It's almost time for the moment of truth.

The countdown to the world's funniest joke.

But first, let's start with the world's worst jokes . . .

The world's worst jokes

 If I eat three cakes in the morning and three for tea . . . what will I have?
A tummy ache

 Why were the rabbits eating the motorway?
It was a duel cabbageway!

3 What's green and likes snow?
Ski-weed

2 What does pride go before?
Of lions!

And the gold medal for the World's Worst Joke goes to:

Knock Knock
Who's there?
Boo
Boo who?
Don't cry

Sadly, being the world's worst joke, we suspect that many people did.

Having dispensed with the worst, it's time for the best. The ten funniest jokes in the world. In reverse order, of course . . .

10 Bob received a parrot for his birthday. The parrot was fully grown, with a very bad attitude and worse vocabulary. Every other word was an expletive; those that weren't expletives were, to say the least, rude. Bob tried to change the bird's attitude by constantly saying polite words, playing soft music, anything he could think of. Nothing worked. He yelled at the bird, and the bird got worse. He shook the bird, and the bird got madder and more rude. Finally, in a moment of desperation, Bob put the parrot in the freezer. For a few moments he heard the bird swearing, squawking, kicking and screaming and then, suddenly, there was absolute quiet. Bob was frightened that he might have actually hurt the bird, and quickly opened the freezer door. The parrot calmly stepped out on to Bob's extended arm and said: 'I'm sorry that I offended you with my language and my actions, and I ask your forgiveness. I will endeavour to correct my behaviour.' Bob was astounded at the changes in the bird's attitude and was about to ask what had changed him, when the parrot continued: 'May I ask what the chicken did?'

This joke was submitted by Diane, 51, a computer programmer from Tasmania.

This joke was sent to me on email by a colleague Peter, and he can't remember where he got it from. The reason I liked it was because my son had a cockatiel called Pedro. He needed so much attention, he was a bit of a nuisance, so I loved this joke about a parrot getting it's come-uppance.

 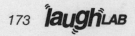

9 A man took his Rottweiler to the vet and said to him:
'My dog's cross-eyed. Is there anything you can do
for it?'
'Well,' said the vet, 'let's have a look at him.' So he
picks the dog up by the ears and has a good look at
its eyes.
'Well,' says the vet, 'I'm going to have to put him
down.'
'Just because he's cross-eyed?' said the man.
'No, because he's heavy,' said the vet.

8 This guy runs home and bursts in yelling: 'Pack your bags, sweetheart, I've just won the lottery, all six numbers!'

She says: 'Oh wonderful! Should I pack for the beach or the mountains?'

He replies: 'I don't care . . . just pack & shove off!'

This was submitted by Isabelle, 30, a Personnel Officer from London.

I think a friend e-mailed the joke to me and I like the joke because it's short enough that you don't have time to guess what the punchline is before you hear it, but just descriptive enough to build up the joyful scene in your mind before the unexpected hits you. Also, having studied languages, it occurs to me that it's a joke that would work in any language and the lottery is a pretty world-wide phenomenon which almost everyone can relate to.

7 A man calls the fire department and yells: 'Help, help! My house is on fire!'

The operator says: 'Calm down. How do we get there?'

The man says: 'Don't you have those big red trucks anymore?'

This came from Marky, 47, from Oregon in the US.

I heard it on TV many years ago. I like it because it's a concise play on verbal comprehension. I've responded with similar skewed understanding to simple queries myself – so I can identify with the joke, and laugh at myself . . .

Sixth came that classic weasel joke:

At the parade, the colonel noticed something unusual going on and asked the major: 'Major Barry, what the devil's wrong with Sergeant Jones' platoon? They seem to be all twitching and jumping about.'
'Well, sir,' says Major Barry after a moment of observation. 'There seems to be a weasel chomping on his privates.'

5 A magician worked on a cruise ship. The audience was different each week, so he did the same tricks over and over again. One problem: The captain's parrot saw the shows each week and began to figure out how the magician did every trick. Once he understood, he started shouting in the middle of the show: 'Look, it's not the same hat!' 'Look, he's hiding the flowers under the table!' 'Hey, why are all the cards the ace of spades?'

The magician was furious but couldn't do anything. It was, after all, the captain's parrot. Then, during a fierce storm, the ship sank. The magician found himself on a piece of wood in the middle of the sea with, as fate would have it, the parrot.

They stared at each other with hatred but did not utter a word. This went on for a day, and then another and then another. Finally on the fourth day, the parrot could not hold back: 'OK, I give up. Where's the ship?'

This joke came from Tady, 26, from the appropriately named Limerick in Ireland:

It's just so simple. I like all jokes, especially anything that makes me laugh out loud. But I think one of the best things is I had never heard it before. It was new. Sometimes you meet your friends and someone tells you a joke and you realise you've heard it before. I had NEVER heard this before and I laughed long, heartily and out loud . . . That's what makes a great joke and that's what made this one so funny. Glad that so many people enjoyed it!

I want to die peacefully in my sleep like my grandfather. Not screaming and yelling like his passengers.

The bronze medal went to:

A man and his wife were having some problems at home and were giving each other the silent treatment. The next week the man realized that he would need his wife to wake him at 5:00 a.m. for an early flight to Sydney. Not wanting to be the first to break the silence, he finally wrote on a piece of paper, 'Please wake me at 5:00 a.m.' The next morning the man woke up, only to discover it was 9:00 a.m., and that he had missed his flight. Furious, he was about to go and see why his wife hadn't awakened him when he noticed a piece of paper by the bed. It said. 'It's 5:00 a.m. wake up.'

The silver went to our original winner from the December analysis:

Sherlock Holmes and Dr Watson were going camping. They pitched their tent under the stars and went to sleep. Sometime in the middle of the night Holmes woke Watson up and said: 'Watson, look up at the stars, and tell me what you see.'
Watson replied: 'I see millions and millions of stars.'
Holmes said: 'And what do you deduce from that?'
Watson replied: 'Well, if there are millions of stars, and if even a few of those have planets, it's quite likely there are some planets like Earth out there. And if there are a few planets like Earth out there, there might also be life.'
And Holmes said: 'Watson, you idiot, it means that somebody stole our tent.'

*laugh*LAB

So, Holmes and Watson were just pipped to the post by another joke.

The winning joke was submitted by Gurpal, a 31-year-old psychiatrist from Manchester in the UK. He told LaughLab that:

I like the joke as it makes people feel better, because it reminds them that there is always someone out there who is doing something more stupid than themselves.

So, now the time has come to reveal the world's funniest joke.

Drum roll . . .

The funniest joke in the world:

A couple of New Jersey hunters are out in the woods when one of them falls to the ground. He doesn't seem to be breathing, his eyes are rolled back in his head. The other guy whips out his cell phone and calls the emergency services. He gasps to the operator: 'My friend is dead! What can I do?'
The operator, in a calm soothing voice says: 'Just take it easy. I can help. First, let's make sure he's dead.'
There is a silence, then a shot is heard. The guy's voice comes back on the line. He says: 'OK, now what?'

It's a truly great gag. It works across many different countries, appeals to men and women, and young and old alike. It involves all three tickle theories – we feel superior to the stupid hunter, realise the incongruity of him misunderstanding the operator and it helps us to laugh about our concerns over our own mortality. Not only that – it is 105 words long – almost the perfect length for a joke!

The last laugh

So there we have it. The results of the world's largest ever experiment into jokes and laughter.

Over 300,000 people from all around the world visited LaughLab to submit their favourite jokes, and tell us what they thought about other people's submissions.

With their help, LaughLab revealed a huge amount about humour. The project discovered why we find certain jokes funnier than others, why some gags make men guffaw and women groan, and how our sense of humour changes as we grow older. Along the way we have also uncovered some of the greatest gags from many different countries, and found the world's best and worst jokes.

We would like to thank everyone who took part in the experiment for providing us with some hilarious jokes and fascinating data. We hope that you have had as much fun reading this book as we had carrying out the experiment.

We thought it was appropriate to leave you with a joke that was submitted by one of our youngest jokesters, Cameron, age 6, from Scotland:

What does the sea do when it's time to leave the beach?
It waves goodbye.

Goodbye.

Notes

1 Berk, L.S., Tan, S.A., Berk, D.B., & Eby, W.C. (1991). *Immune system changes during associated laughing,* Clinical Research, 39, 124A.

2 Fry, W.F., & Rader, C. (1977). 'The respiratory components of mirthful laughter.' *The Journal of Biological Psychology,* 19, 39–50.

3 Described in Funes, M. (2000). *Laughing Matters: Live Creatively with Laughter.* Dublin: Newleaf.

4 Trice, A.D. & Price-Greathouse, J. (1986). 'Joking under the drill: A validity study of the coping humour scale.' *Journal of Social Behaviour and Personality,* 1, 265–266.

5 Binsted, K., & Ritchie, G. (1997). 'Computational rules for punning riddles.' *Humour: International Journal of Humour Research,* 10(l).

6 Asimov, I. (1994). *The Complete Stories,* Volume 1. London: Harper Collins.

7 Provine, R.R. (2000). *Laughter: A Scientific Investigation.* New York: Viking.

8 Harris, C.R. (1999). 'The mystery of ticklish laughter.' *American Scientist,* 87, 344–351.

9 Provine, R.R. (2000). *Laughter: A Scientific Investigation.* New York: Viking.

 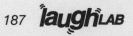

10 Funes, M. (2000). *Laughing Matters: Live Creatively with Laughter*. Dublin: Newleaf.

11 Martin, R.A. & Kuiper, N.A. (1999). 'Daily occurrence of humour: relationships with age, gender and Type A personality.' *Humour: International Journal of Humour Research*, 12, 355–384.

12 Davies, C. (1986). 'Jewish jokes, anti-Semitic jokes and Hebredonian jokes.' In A. Ziv (Ed) *Jewish Humour*. Tel Aviv: Papyrus Publishing House.

13 Kuiper, N.A., Martin, R.F., & Dance, K.A. (1992). 'Sense of humour and enhanced quality of life.' *Personality and Individual Differences*, 13, 1273–1283.

14 Ruch, W. & Carrell, A. (1998). 'Trait cheerfulness and the sense of humour.' *Personality and Individual Differences*, 24, 551–558.

15 Argyle, M. (2001). *The Psychology of Happiness*. London: Routledge.

16 Chapman, A.J. (1976). 'Social aspects of humorous laughter'. In A.J. Chapman & H.C. Foot (Eds.) *Humour and Laughter: Theory, Research and Applications*. Chichester, UK: Wiley.

17 Avner, Z., Gorenstein, E. & Mons, A. (1986). 'Adolescents' evaluation of teachers using disparaging humour.' *Educational Psychology*, 6, 37–44.

18 Argyle, M. (1989). *The Social Psychology of Work*. London: Penguin.

19 Deckers, W.H., & Rotondo, D.M. (1999). 'Use of humour at work: predictors and implications.' *Psychological Reports*, 84, 961–968.

20 Lundy, D.E., Tan, J., & Cunningham, M.R. (1998). 'Heterosexual romantic preferences: the importance of humour and physical attractiveness for different types of relationships.' *Personal Relationships*, 5, 311–325.

21 Panksepp, J., & Burgdorf, J. (1999). 'Laughing rats? Playful tickling arouses high-frequency ultrasonic chirping in young rodents.' In S. Hameroff, D. Chambers and A. Kaziak (Eds.), *Toward a Science of Consciousness III*. Cambridge, MA: MIT Press.

22 Janus, S.S. (1975). 'The great comedians: personality and other factors.' *American Journal of Psychoanalysis*, 35, 169–174.

23 Hinsz, V.B. & Tomhave, J.A. (1991). 'Smile and (Half) the World Smiles with You, Frown and You Frown Alone.' *Personality and Social Psychology Bulletin*, 17(5), 586–592.

24 Rankin, A.M. & Philip, P.J. (1963). 'An epidemic of laughing in the Bukoba district of Tanganyika.' *The Central African Journal of Medicine*, 9, 167–170.

25 Roach, M. (1996). 'Can you laugh your stress away?' *Health*, September 1996.

26 The information in this section is from: Provine, R.R. (2000). *Laughter: A Scientific Investigation*. New York: Viking.

27 Brownell, H.H. & Hardner, H. (1988).
'Neuropsychological insights into humour.' In J. Durant
& J. Miller (Eds.) *Laughing Matters: A serious look at
humour*. Harlow, UK: Longman Scientific and
Technical. 17–35.